SERMONS

PREACHED IN THE

Second Church, Dorchester,

BY

JAMES H. MEANS.

Boston:
PRINTED BY ALFRED MUDGE AND SON.
1865.

Contents.

TO THE SECOND CHURCH AND SOCIETY,

DORCHESTER:

It is the wish of your Pastor to place upon your tables this little volume, to speak for him while for a season his voice is silent. It is made up of a few sermons, selected for no special excellence, but simply as presenting practical truths, adapted to different classes, and such as a Pastor would desire those committed to his spiritual charge to keep in mind.

The first may remind the unconverted of their danger. The second and the third may help them to understand the way of escape, and also show to Christians that glorious fulness of Divine grace which the writer has never wearied of declaring. The fourth may indicate the spirit in which all should live and labor for Christ, even when cheered with but little apparent success. The fifth is an attempt to illustrate the beauty and power of the inspired Word; a volume which ever grows more dear, and unfolds a richer meaning the longer it is studied. The sixth is addressed to all, as a persuasive to interweave religion with the whole business of this life; while the last carries the thoughts from the present to that higher life which is to come, to which all the truths and ordinances of the Gospel are intended to lead.

There is no peculiar novelty in the treatment of these themes, and they are offered only to those bound to the writer by friendly ties; especially to those, affection to whom has sprung up during a happy Pastorate of sixteen and a half years, and has been deepened by most kind and generous favors recently shown.

Precious memories of joys and sorrows, which we have shared, and common hopes reaching on into eternity, bind us together; and though separated for a time, if, as I have been assured, I shall have your "prayers, fervent and faithful," and your "eyes will wander with" me, "and wishfully await" my "coming," no less earnest shall be my supplications for your prosperity, — no less glad to me the hour which permits me again to speak to you of the inexhaustible wonders and glories of "the truth as it is in Jesus."

J. H. M.

Dorchester, January, 1865.

The Office of Fear in Religion.

KNOWING, THEREFORE, THE TERROR OF THE LORD, WE PERSUADE MEN. II. *Corinthians*, v.: 11.

THERE IS NO FEAR IN LOVE, BUT PERFECT LOVE CASTETH OUT FEAR. I. *John*, iv.: 18.

THE truth is often best stated in paradoxes. It has two sides, and the right impression comes from seeing both. The fulness of the Scripture is often thus exhibited, and there are passages which seem contradictory because the view given of the truth is so complete.

Paul and James are often arrayed against each other on the subject of faith and works. Their words are directly at variance. One says, "A man is not justified by the works of the law, but by the faith of Christ;" the other, "Ye see that by works a man is justified, and not by faith only." Yet both are right; the one having chief regard to the ground of justification, the other to its evidence; and the truth is seen full-orbed, by the combination of the two.

So in our texts, it is possible to array Paul and John in opposition. The former recognizes "the terror of the Lord" as a constraining motive which he felt, and which he used. The other, exalting love, seems even to reproach those who are led by fear; declares that love casts it out, and that "he that feareth is not made perfect in love."

Yet again we say, both speak truly. The impulse of fear in our religious life is legitimate and necessary; yet there is a stage of Christian development in which we are lifted above it and swayed by a higher principle.

Let me now endeavor to illustrate these positions.

In the outset, it is to be observed that the influence of fear, or the apprehension of evil, largely regulates the daily course of all. How constantly does this underlie and prompt the activities of life. That foresight, prudence, caution, essential to a well-regulated course, what is it but a watchful forecasting of possible dangers and labor to avert them?

It is an original impulse of nature, without which the mind is defective, and one is unable to plan rightly. It is a motive continually appealed to in lesser and in great emergencies. It keeps us busy at our daily toil; and when the greatest power of citizenship is to be exercised, and one chosen to hold the destinies of a nation in his hand, on both sides the effort is to awaken fear as to the results which would follow the election of the candidate opposed. Thus universal is this sentiment, as a principle of action among men.

Now notice further how steadily it is appealed to in the Bible. We should expect it would be. How could a book designed to affect the conduct of men, fail to touch one of the most strongly vibrating chords in the human breast? From the opening chapters to those which close the Revelation, we find men addressed on this side of their sensibilities. When man sinned, the first voice that broke harshly on the peacefulness of Eden was a summons to judgment: "Where art thou? What is this that thou hast done?" Then followed that curse upon the man, the woman, and the earth, which has never been taken off, and beneath which we toil and groan to-day.

I need but remind you how large a portion of the messages of the prophets were rebukes and threatenings; how the lurid flames of Sinai ever burn and flash behind them, and Jehovah is seen going forth wrapped in the clouds of a terrible and avenging majesty. Nor is it otherwise in the New Testament. Divine grace is made more prominent, but the sterner attributes are not hidden, still less denied. "God is love," we read; and yet, also, "He is a consuming fire." "It is a fearful thing to fall into the hands of the living God." The New Testament not only maintains the old declarations of the Divine holiness, and justice, and omniscience, and human accountability, with unabated force, but it brings out more distinctly, it enforces more impressively, with greater vividness of imagery, and the direct authority of the Son of God himself, the fact of a day of judgment, and of future retribution.

The principle of fear, then, has unmistakably its place among the motives of the Gospel; it belongs to the new as well as the old dispensation. Christ appealed to it; and it is enough for the disciple to be as his Lord. In regard to these highest interests of the soul, we are to use that forecast which belongs to all rational action, and to despise that presumption which mocks at the thought of danger.

But this leads to another point worthy of more full consideration. *What is the precise use and efficacy of this motive of fear in religion?* Let us trace its operations.

First, *it arouses men.* It must be remembered that the state in which we all are found is not a condition of moral soundness, but of disease. Sin has infected us, and courses like a poison through our frames. One of the most marked symptoms of this disorder of the soul is a lethargy, insensibility, somnolence. We hear the most animating, startling truths as though we heard them not. The Gospel must therefore be presented in its most forcible form, with images most distinct, and facts most impressive. Soft words are pleasant, but they lull to a deeper slumber. The sleeper needs to be awakened, and we must break in upon him, even rudely, with the cry of danger. If he sleep on, he dies.

These alarming truths, which are so objected to, are the means God has given to wake up the careless and the presumptuous. One skilled in mental analysis has given this challenge: "I ask for a solitary, decisive instance of conversion, in which no influence of God's threatenings has been felt." He would not deny the efficacy of the Divine goodness; but the deepest conviction of this springs from a view of the deserved judgments which have been turned aside. It is grace triumphing over wrath, which melts and subdues.

In the Scriptural examples of conversion, certainly, the power of this motive is manifest. It was when the jailer trembled that he asked "the great question"; it was when the three thousand were "pricked in their hearts," that the blessing of Pentecost came. This was the beginning of the work of God in their souls, as it has been in the souls of uncounted thousands since.

There never was a revival in which the sterner attributes of God and the fearfulness of the sinner's just doom were not plainly revealed. This may not be all that is needed, but it is an essential part. The carelessly secure must be aroused, attention drawn to those things which concern their peace, the veil by which their eyes are blinded must be torn away, and their ears unstopped to hear the alarm-bell of the clock of destiny.

Again, these awakening truths *are needed to restrain men.* Sinners are rushing to destruction; we would hold them back. How? By speaking smoothly; by dwelling only on the mercy and love of God; by declaring the fulness of the Saviour's expiation and the freeness of the Spirit's grace? These truths, glorious as they are, are often perverted; and men thinking to repent and find acceptance at any time are at ease in sin — all the while plunging deeper in guilt and straying farther upon God. You must have something else to restrain them.

Let God, therefore, be seen upon His high and glorious throne, watching each one whom He has made, searching the heart and its real hidden motives, remembering every offence He sees, abhorring, from the necessity of His pure nature, all manner of evil. Let the day be anticipated, when each one must stand before that holy and just God and give account of all his deeds; when there shall be nothing hidden, and no sin lightly esteemed; when the irreversible sentence shall be pronounced, and guilt unrepented of and unforgiven must be the ruin of the soul.

Here is what will balance the attractions of sin. Man is called to weigh the momentary pleasure of self-indulgence against this prolonged misery. Even one given up to selfishness may well ask whether, while seeking so eagerly earthly goods, he is not perilling interests and sacrificing good far greater. It is the old question renewed, "What shall it profit a man if he gain the whole world and lose his own soul?" Nay, we seem to hear the echo of a still more ancient warning: "Rejoice, O young man, in thy youth, and let thine heart cheer thee in the days of thy youth, and walk in the ways of thine heart, and in the sight of thine eyes; but know thou that for all these things God will bring thee into judgment."

Is there no power in this to check even the ebullition of passion? Are those things to be chosen or hated, which drag after them such fearful ruin? Is that a path of pleasure which leads to endless woe? If such truths — if Divine warnings against unbelief and impenitence, as leading to sure destruction, cannot restrain, what barrier can be set up to stay the rush of the multitudes in the broad and downward path?

Further, these stern truths *are fitted to impress deeply a sense of the evil of sin.* Indeed, without them, I see not how any such impression could be produced. That which we treat lightly cannot be made to seem very bad. In the family, you may lecture daily on the enormity of disobedience, but unless you deal with it as a grave offence, your words go for nothing. In the state, the public conscience is trained by the penalties attached to crime. The fact that the extreme sentence of the law follows murder, hedges human life around with peculiar sacredness in the view of all. The man tempted to destroy it is not merely afraid of being hung, — he feels a dread of the deed, the heinousness of which can only be expressed by such a penalty. The idea is driven into his obtuse understanding by the terror of the law, that shedding man's blood is a fearful sin.

So, under the government of God, there is a necessity for a stern system of judgment and penalties; or transgressions, even of the highest law, will appear trivial. A gently treated rebellion, whether against man or God, is a legalized rebellion. How can you convince one that in wandering away from God and setting up his will against the Divine authority, he is doing what is a foul offence, if the very Being offended is ready to pass it by almost unnoticed? Man is inclined to make light of his sin; the world will not judge him harshly: what shall wake his conscience to the needed work of contrition and repentance, but the threatening voice of God?

He hears it, demanding, What is this which thou hast done? and the startling question echoes through all the chambers of the soul. He wakes to a consciousness that he has defied supreme power, insulted and injured infinite grace, trampled on a law of perfect holiness, broken up the order of the universe, — has, as far as his own act could do it, dethroned God.

At the same time he is made to feel the hopelessness of resistance. God and man stand in opposition; but what a contrast. On the one side, might; on the other, impotence. The thing formed defying Him who formed it. What hope is there, save in submission? The Omnipotent can crush his foes; the All-Holy and Just will uphold His government and throne, though worlds sink in ruin. Sin is not only heinous; it is mad presumption,—evil in its nature, only evil in its consequences.

Nothing but these truths of accountability and judgment can thus turn his thoughts to the enormity of his guilt; nothing but the holding up of each offence before God, and in the light of eternity, can make its true, foul character appear. This can, as thousands of broken hearts can testify. "By the law is the knowledge of sin."

But this is by no means all that the soul needs. Out of these convictions of guilt and ill-desert, rise longings for deliverance. The distressed sinner looks anxiously for relief; and thus fear accomplishes its final and highest office, *in shutting men up to the Gospel;* leading them to the entrance of that path, where it is itself lost in love.

Oftentimes, this result is reached through the efforts to which men are stimulated to escape the consequences of sin. In the outset, these take the form of labors of penance and self-righteousness. Be it so. If one, self-condemned, wishes to try the experiment of saving himself, let him.

If he thinks that reformation in his own strength is better than repentance and renewal by the Spirit, let him see how long it will take to bring his heart and life into exact conformity to the will of God.

There can be but one issue to such a trial with any truly earnest and candid man. He will be constantly coming short and ever dissatisfied. He may grow attenuated as a shadow through his penances, but he will find, like Luther in the convent, that this is not the way of peace. He may surmount one evil, and another, but as he presses on, "Alps on Alps still rise"; one elevation gained only shows higher and more difficult summits unscaled before him, and he sees that strength will give out, and life will end, before the height he aims at is reached. What shall he do? Unable to save himself, he needs a Saviour; can such be found?

Here the Gospel comes in. The penalties of the law are threatened, not yet inflicted; nay, understand this also, He who threatens does not desire to inflict them. A way of escape has been provided. The innocent comes from heaven to suffer for the guilty. Christ takes our sins upon him that whosoever believeth may be freely forgiven.

How this changes the position of men. There is hope for the guiltiest. Those terrors, which alone would arouse enmity, or drive to despair, now humble and convict, yet soften and subdue. While God invites, they urge to the acceptance of the invitation. The Divine countenance, stern with the awful majesty of holiness, yet now irradiated by the smile of reconciliation, becomes unutterably attractive. The soul, already convinced of sin, melts before the power of the Divine tenderness. It was needful that there should have been a work of alarm and conviction; but if the humbled heart has been thus prepared to embrace a Saviour, the law may silence its thunders, and the Gospel whisper peace.

Thus love springs up under the combined power of the severity and goodness of God, both needed for the effect. It is the sign of a new life of reconciliation and friendship. There is no fear in it; our guilt, which alone made God terrible to us, is removed and cancelled when we believe in Christ; the happy child rests in confidence in his Father's arms; and "perfect love casteth out fear." The bow of promise arches over the departing clouds.

These truths teach us the benevolence of those threatenings and stern doctrines, of which so many are unwilling to hear. Why has God made known the responsibilities and the perils of sinners? Is it not because this is the very way — the only way — to rouse men to avoid them? Suppose He had left them to all the natural delusions of flattering hearts, to live and die unwarned; and then had confronted them with the undeclared consequences. How impossible such a course must have been to a God of mercy.

And what is the dictate of kindness, as to our own duty? Loving our neighbors, shall we declare the truth plainly to them, or keep silent? What matters it what they wish to hear? Shall we let the drunkard drink because the cup is pleasant, and snatch not the knife from the hand of the suicide because he wishes to use it? Can we, then, suffer men to destroy their soul's life through ignorance of the truth? It is love which opens the lips to reason of sin and a judgment; and the warmer the love, the more faithful the unveiling of the whole truth.

If we shrink from the duty; if the parent dreads to warn his children plainly — if the preacher is tempted not to "mention hell to ears polite" and fastidious, let our affection for those endangered banish the weak cowardice, and make us honest with them and true to their souls.

We also learn the proper way in which these warnings should be received. They are to be welcomed, not evaded or denied. Let us know what our situation really is. Let us know the worst, for then we shall see what we have to do. If the evil were past remedy, it might be said, Torment us not before the time; but, thank God, while there is life there is hope, — One mighty to save; and we want to see the very opening of the abyss, that our sluggish steps may be quickened in the path of safety.

But some have said, We will not be frightened into religion. Is it, then, unmanly to see real dangers and provide against them? A timorous trouble about imaginary evils may be foolish; but if a house were burning, and the flames encircling your chamber, and consuming the stairway, would you refuse to be frightened into leaving?

It is simply rational, — the highest reason and the truest manhood, — to look facts in the face; to take well-grounded warning; to provide against all threatening perils, and most carefully against the worst. Therefore, we hold up these truths, and call on you who are every day commendably watching against calamity, with equal foresight and wisdom to seek pardon and eternal life.

Let each one now ask himself: What is the influence of the warnings and threatenings of God's word upon me?

You may be a Christian. Still you need to keep constantly in mind what sin is, and to have an ever-deepening sense of its heinousness. The discipline of those truths which humble and abase is needed every day you live. Never ought any of us to forget from what we have been delivered. We read the curses of the law, and if through abounding grace no more we tremble, the louder let our exultant thanksgivings ascend, and the more hearty and entire be our consecration. We read them; and while we rejoice in deliverance, we feel that the place which belongs to us is at God's feet; we are not worthy to be called His children — let Him use us as servants to do His bidding.

Thus, too, shall we be led to magnify with fullest appreciation the grace of God in Jesus Christ. They love the most, who feel that they have had much forgiven.

If you are not accepted and pardoned through the Redeemer, can you sit quietly, exposed to the just wrath of God? Is there a charm in the pleasures of the world, which may end so soon? Is seeming wealth and prosperity aught but a delusive and fleeting show? Can you be indifferent to these threatenings, as though God spake in vain? Did He drive out our fallen parents from Eden; did He come down in the flaming clouds of Sinai; did He send the long line of warning prophets and apostles, aye, and his only begotten Son, speaking plainer and more fearful words than any other, and does your insensible heart resist every appeal?

Time rolls on. Never,—never stood you so near to the judgment as at this hour; never, therefore, had you so much reason to listen to the expostulation sounding from God's word, "Turn ye, turn ye, for why will ye die?"

The Conversion of St. Paul.

AND, AS HE JOURNEYED, HE CAME NEAR DAMASCUS: AND SUDDENLY THERE SHINED ROUND ABOUT HIM A LIGHT FROM HEAVEN; AND HE FELL TO THE EARTH, AND HEARD A VOICE SAYING UNTO HIM, SAUL, SAUL, WHY PERSECUTEST THOU ME? AND HE SAID, WHO ART THOU, LORD? AND THE LORD SAID, I AM JESUS, WHOM THOU PERSECUTEST: IT IS HARD FOR THEE TO KICK AGAINST THE PRICKS. AND HE, TREMBLING AND ASTONISHED, SAID, LORD, WHAT WILT THOU HAVE ME TO DO? *Acts*, ix.: 3 — 6.

THERE is no conflict going on upon the earth so momentous as that between good and evil in the human soul, and no victory so blessed is ever won as when holiness triumphs there.

The great change by which one passes from death to life is the more worthy of thought and inquiry, because it must, according to our Saviour's teaching, be experienced by all before they can be prepared for heaven. "Except a man be born again, he can not see the kingdom of God."

This change is, in its inner nature and essence, the same in all. Heart answereth to heart. All have been smitten down in the same corruption and ruin; all ransomed by one Redeemer, and needing renewal from the same Spirit: so that we may take one case like this of the apostle Paul, and use it to illustrate the nature of all true conversions.

The circumstances may be peculiar, the succession of feelings different from what it has been in others, the manifestations of a changed heart different also; in all these outward respects there is an endless variety, and new converts may not safely make the experience of others a standard for their own; but when we look beneath at the real nature of the change, we find it always essentially the same. We need the same renewal of heart which Paul experienced. The Spirit who regenerated him must awaken us to a new life, and that life must be to us as it was to him, — a life of submission, and prayer, and love.

Let us, then, carefully examine the story of Paul's conversion, presented in the text and the connected Scriptures, as illustrating the nature of this spiritual change.

Thus viewed, it reminds us, First, that *the conversion of the soul is effected by the power of God.* The first and the deepest impression made by the narrative is of the supernatural agency exerted.

The flashing light, the heavenly voice, the vision of glory; these make the scene most solemn and grand. No one reads the record believingly without feeling that God came very near to that traveller to Damascus; that it was a Divine hand which arrested, and Omnipotence which subdued him. It was, we are told, the accomplishment of a Divine purpose. "He is a chosen vessel unto me to bear my name before the Gentiles."

Now, in this Paul's case was not peculiar. The interposition of God was not more real than in any other case, though it was more plainly seen. Surely God can come in the darkness, as well as in the light; with silence, in the still hour, as well as with the trembling and roar of the thunder. At times He reveals himself visibly, but certainly not to lead us to deny His invisible presence. He chose to give a striking demonstration of His agency in the conversion of this eminent believer, that when He was not so clearly seen at such a crisis in life, men might still believe and feel Him to be near.

The Scripture constantly ascribes this change to His power. "Born of the Spirit" is the phrase our Saviour was pleased to use; "born, not of blood, nor of the will of the flesh, nor of the will of man, but of God," is the discriminating statement we find elsewhere.

Experience also confirms this. We need not

ask for light and sounds from heaven, and visions which smite blind and destroy all power, to tell us of a present God. When the conscience cannot rest, when sins long forgotten throng back to view, when no pleasures can charm, and no force of will keep the mind steady, when the strong man writhes as in the grasp of a stronger, when he feels as he never felt before, speaks as he never spoke, prays, turns to his neglected Bible, tastes not his wonted food; what matters it, whether God appeared to Him in the way, or only makes His presence felt instead of seen?

Not always, indeed, are these tokens of God so marked; but they are so with sufficient frequency to confirm the teaching of the Word, that conversion is always a change accompanied by Divine agency; that he who would receive the grace must look upward, and in all his strivings seek and depend upon heavenly aid.

This, however, is not the whole truth; and the narrative before us teaches, Secondly, that *conversion includes the free and earnest activity of man.* The influences to which Paul was subjected were overpowering, but they did not destroy reason or will. He trembled and was astonished, but was not smitten into inaction.

On the contrary, we believe his mind never acted with such sublime force and determination.

His greatness was seen in his self-possession. There were no passionate outcries. He faced the mystery of that vision, and calmly asked its meaning. "Who art thou, Lord?" What entire self-command the inquiry showed. And when the answer came: "I am Jesus, whom thou persecutest," that great soul, whose energies were only driven to a focus by the appalling revelations around, centred the decision of a lifetime in one mighty act of self-surrender; and asking "What wilt thou have me to do?" laid itself down at the feet of the Redeemer, at once and forever.

Notwithstanding all the signs of supernatural agency which attended the change, never has there been a convert who more certainly turned himself to the Lord, and was active in the momentous hour.

So when he prayed, and when in that three days' fasting and darkness, he communed with himself, reviewed the past, anticipated the future, repeated his consecration; was there ever a time, think you, when he was more earnest in thought, emotion, purpose? The outward eye was closed, that the inward vision might be the clearer; and the entire crowded years of his wonderful ministry were but the acting out of the vows of those silent hours.

Let us not think that God will do our work for us. He holds to a division of labor. He makes all the objects of creation to fulfil some office—not, indeed, in independence of Himself, but with His coöperation. Even the plant works in raising and distributing the sap, inhaling the atmosphere, nourishing and ripening its seed. Man, in his relations to this world, must sow and reap, must hew the wood and build the house, and fashion his raiment; or he will go hungry, and shelterless, and naked. God provides,—God helps continually, but leaves him his own work.

So in spiritual things. No heavenly warning or aid, though it transcend all common experience, though it be by special revelation, can supersede the activity of man. The awakened, convicted sinner must repent, believe, obey, by his own act; God working in him, while he works. The manifestation of God may prostrate him to the earth; but it is possible for him to lie there hardening his heart, resisting the truth, and to rise unsubmissive and unsubdued. Those who yield become trophies of God's mercy; those who will not yield, monuments of his wrath.

This explains the contest we sometimes see. The battle rages, it waxes hot. God is pressing with motives and mysterious influences—man resists. God will not let him go—he struggles to be free. Deeper, more tender becomes the beseeching voice, more piercing his distress; he must submit, that will end the strife — God is waiting for that, to bless him with peace. Let him cast himself, helpless, ruined, guilty, upon the free mercy of his Saviour; let him devote himself to that Lord, in the entire consecration of every power to His service, and in that moment his new life begins; he is accepted — he is saved.

In the third place, this history of Paul shows us *how speedily the work of conversion may be accomplished.* Many associate with the passing of a soul from death to life the idea of a prolonged struggle. That such a conflict sometimes occurs cannot be denied, but it is not necessary. Certainly we see nothing like it here. So sudden — so entirely unexpected was the change in Paul, we can only say it was as a dream.

He arose, on the morning of that most eventful day, intent only on persecuting the saints of God. He pressed on, unresting even under the noontide rays of an Eastern sun, so eager was he to accomplish his errand of slaughter. Half the day had been filled with threatenings and purposes of malignity; yet, ere that sun went down, which shone on him in all the fierceness of his bigoted wrath, he was to be numbered among the followers of Christ, and his name written, never to be blotted out, in the book of life. Perhaps not an hour passed — a close adherence to the record might even lead us to think it only a few minutes — from the time when he was arrested in his course, until he had submitted, wholly and forever, to his new Master.

Nor is there anything in the nature of conversion which would be inconsistent with this view. Of course, Paul had often heard of Jesus, of his life, his miracles, his teachings, his death; he knew how Stephen and others regarded Him — how the dying martyr had committed to Him his soul, and fallen asleep. It was only necessary that, renouncing his vain confidence in Judaism, he should show the same faith in Christ; and the moment his eyes were opened to see the Divine glory of this persecuted One, he could do this.

If salvation were of works, — if the requirement had been, that he should have presented himself strong, tried, experienced, having attained, having done some great thing, being what he afterwards became; — why then, indeed, poor Paul would have had I know not how many struggles, or how long delay; but since the terms were — as, thank God, they still are — simply to believe, and take grace as a gift; not to make himself clean, but to come in all his vileness and be cleansed, there needed not a moment's preparation or a moment's waiting — only the instantaneous assent of a needy, trusting soul.

Can you see anything that Paul would have

gained, or how he would have been in any better position to receive Christ, had he withheld that submission on the road, and said, Lead me to Damascus, then leave me; I will meditate on these things, I will pray, I will confer with Christians there, and then I will decide?

Yet this is what is often done. Who thinks of submitting at the first call in the sanctuary? Those most moved are thinking of hastening home to their closets, and there beginning the process of giving their hearts to Christ.

But why not do it at once? The Gospel always presses to an immediate surrender. Cast away the weapons of your rebellion, as the defeated in a battle instantly yield. There is no need of any other place, or of any process of conversion whatever,—believe, submit; even a moment's delay is dangerous, for it is continuance in sin.

It should be added here, that a distinction is made between one's becoming a Christian, and attaining the consciousness that he is one. We regard Paul as converted when he asked, "What wilt Thou have me to do?" because the inquiry showed the submissive spirit of a true disciple. Whether he then thought of himself as a Christian, may be doubted. Those days in which his eyes were blinded may have been days of darkness to his spirit also, and the touch and cheering salutation of Ananias may have carried light to both body and soul. We know from the writings of the apostle, that at some time his sins, especially as a persecutor, were set in order before him. He who called himself chief among sinners, must have known the horrors of a soul crushed by a sense of guilt; and it may have been that while his submission was instantaneous, and his acceptance with God, yet the peace and hope, following a consciousness of that acceptance, entered only by degrees into his soul. We do not assert this — only say it may have been — to remind you that conversion is one thing, and the peace which follows it another; so that we are not to be mainly anxious to find peace and joy, but to do what God requires, — that is, trust in His mercy in Christ, and give ourselves up to His service forever.

In the fourth place, this narrative suggests that *one converted will delight in communion with God, and in doing His will.* There is nothing said here about the feelings of Paul, concerning any distress of mind, or any special relief; the evidence of his conversion rests on other, — may I venture to say, — better ground.

The first indication was in that docile and submissive call for guidance, of which, perhaps, enough has been already said. It showed an humbling of pride, a giving up of former plans, and of all self-will, and the choice of Christ to be master — which marked, beyond all contradiction, a new era in his soul's history. For when one is brought to this state, and can in the same way put his soul, his life, all his prospects and his plans, into the hands of Christ, to do with all just what He sees best, then has the man yielded as he is bidden, and Christ takes the precious trust, to keep it unto life eternal. That soul is safe, because none can snatch it from the Saviour's hands.

But this was not the only evidence of Paul's conversion. When Ananias was sent to him, the description given of his state was in these words: "Behold, he prayeth." "Go seek out this Saul of Tarsus — Behold, he prayeth." Had the man never prayed before? This scrupulous Hebrew of the Hebrews, had not he often worshipped in the temple? Yes, as a Pharisee, he had thanked God he was not as other men were; but now, the cry which came with sobs, and groans, and vows, from his broken and contrite spirit, was that other prayer, "Be merciful to me a sinner." It was the cry of one in earnest, the cry of one believing, of one delighting to draw near to God; paying no tithe of a commanded service, but freely pouring out his whole heart before the Lord. So that it could be said of him, in altogether a new sense, "Behold, he prayeth."

Thus every renewed sinner prays. He cannot be a true convert unless he does pray. Conversion is turning to God, and if one truly turns, his heart and voice will speak. "Prayer is the Christian's vital breath," and where there is no breath, there is no life.

This, then, is a most appropriate description of one new born in Christ; "he prayeth." Child of a pious household, he was early taught to pray, and perhaps never ceased from the form, but now there is a new spirit in that nightly devotion. Father of a family, he thought little of being a spiritual father; but now he kneels down with his household around him, and his wondering children hear his strange, tremulous tones as he pleads for them. His oft-frequented closet, loved more and more, and more dearly prized as a place of privilege and joy; the family altar, the place of social Christian conference, the sanctuary where his form, irreverently erect before, is bowed during the service of devotion, and his once wandering eyes are closed: all witness to the change that has passed upon him, and lead many to say, "he prayeth." And they hear of it in heaven, and by that token recognize, and rejoice over a prodigal found.

Lastly, we are here reminded that *conversion brings us into new relations to Christ's disciples.* Not the least affecting among the scenes detailed in this narrative is the inverview between Paul and that "devout man," of whose previous history we know nothing, but whom God sent to the new convert, on an errand of sympathy and aid. Ananias seemed at first afraid to go. He remonstrated, and told the Lord, almost as if He knew it not before, what a persecutor Saul had been. But when the story of that wonderful vision of Jesus was rehearsed to him, and the Lord's purposes revealed, not only did his fears depart, but his very soul went forth in tenderness, and, hastening on his way, he stood before the new convert, blind, enfeebled, helpless, and spoke to him the first words of Christian love he had ever heard: "Brother" — "Brother Saul."

Speak you of the joy of lovers — heart meeting heart? It is precious. God be thanked for giving us this solace in life's pilgrimage. But there is an element of a purer and more heavenly bliss, when gushing sympathy in Christ brings hearts together; a deep and peaceful sense of a unity which God approves, and which is never to be broken; visions rise of sweet fellowship beyond the grave, in the many mansions of our Father's house.

All Christians are one; all living Christians feel themselves to be so when brought together. Rescued from a common ruin, born of the same Spirit, hastening to the same home, the name they give each other, "brethren," is surely more than a name.

What a proof is our "Sabbath Hymn Book" of the fact. There earnest souls have expressed their deepest emotions; and if you open the volume, I cannot tell whether you will come on the composition of Watts, the Congregationalist, or of the Methodist, Wesley, or of some Baptist, or Churchman, or Moravian. Nay, start not if some pious Romanist, like Madame Guyon, speaks to you in kindred tones; or even some canonized saint, like Bernard, or Xavier. It may be a German hymn you open to, or one of France, or Switzerland, or England, or possibly one from an old Greek father of the third century. It matters not — all are one; times, countries, sects are nothing in the presence of those great, central, unchanging verities, which are the chief topics in our praise.

Conversion brings one into this large and goodly fellowship. No one was ever converted to Wesley, or Calvin, or Luther. Who are these but ministers by whom many have believed? They all point to Christ. And when the followers of that one Lord are assembled, and one takes up the heavenly theme, if the refrain of the song, or the plea which rises strong in prayer, or the thought which wails in the expostulation is Christ's love, then all respond, and are of one heart and one mind. Or, when impartial death comes, though it be a Prince in Windsor Castle, on whom disease has laid a mortal hold, he can find no other refuge than that which has been the solace of many a peasant's death-bed,

> "Rock of ages, cleft for me,
> Let me hide myself in Thee,"—

and so, in a common need and common trust, the peasant and the prince are one.

Blessed, then, is this change, which not only brings one to a new individual life, but into new sympathies, wide as the earth, pure as heaven, lasting as eternity.

Such is conversion; and now a question arises which we would address to each one individually: *Have you been converted?* Remember that the signs of this change are marked. It implies submission — the entire surrender of the heart and life to God's control. It shows itself by frequent, earnest prayer, and by love for all true Christians. It will lead to a life, animated like the shining career of Paul, by the mighty impulse of devotion to the Redeemer. If such emotions are not felt, and such signs do not appear, the conclusion must be that your heart has not been renewed.

But what a conclusion is this, when Christ has said, "Ye must be born again." How shall we escape, if His word condemns us? He is the Judge, and what hope is there, save in compliance with His demands?

We look forward to the day when a brighter light than that which shone near Damascus will burst upon us; when we shall look upon Christ seated upon the burning throne, and hear His voice as Paul heard it, demanding how we have treated Him. Are we ready for that approaching scrutiny? Will Christ then see in us those who have opposed, or those who have loved and served him?

Christian Assurance.

I KNOW WHOM I HAVE BELIEVED, AND AM PERSUADED THAT HE IS ABLE TO KEEP THAT WHICH I HAVE COMMITTED UNTO HIM AGAINST THAT DAY. II. *Timothy*, i.: 12.

THIS second epistle to Timothy has that peculiar interest always belonging to the last words of a departing friend. Ties of peculiar tenderness and strength bound Paul to the young disciple whom he had "begotten in the Gospel," and now that he was "ready to be offered, and the time of departure was at hand," he unveiled to him his deepest and most sacred emotions.

Thus we know how a true-souled, mature follower of Christ felt in regard to his highest interests. Cheerfulness, hope, ardent love for Jesus, appear in almost every line, and are especially manifest in the text — "I know whom I have believed, and am persuaded that He is able to keep that which I have committed unto Him against that day."

This is an expression of joyous confidence. The writer was at rest concerning his soul. He had given it into the keeping of another, who was "mighty to save," and so hewas "persuaded" of its safety.

The precise phrase here used is worthy of our special notice. It would be well for us at times to adopt it. If, instead of asking Christians whether they had "assurance" of salvation, we should ask whether they were "persuaded" of their soul's safety, would not more be ready to give assent? Assurance is thought to be equivalent to absolute certainty,—a certainty such that the opposite is impossible; and it seems like presumption in a fallible man, however strong his reasons for confidence, to assert this. No kind of argument, save that based on mathematical demonstration, gives such a certainty. The presumption on which men act, on which they rest with satisfaction, in the ordinary affairs of life comes short of this. We are not absolutely certain of accomplishing any enterprise which we undertake; nor even, when we leave our homes, of returning to them alive. We are sure of success only in the sense of being strongly persuaded of it. This is a kind of assurance, and leads one to say confidently, I know I shall do this or that,—secure this or that result.

If one is disposed to look on the dark side (always a most unprofitable proceeding), he may so exaggerate the uncertainty of life, he may find so many reasons to distrust himself, he may conjure up so many possibilities of failure in every undertaking, that he will not do anything, nor even attempt to do. He may so distress himself with the fallibility of human reason, that he will believe nothing; and so will utterly throw away his life and the powers given to him. We must venture, if we would achieve; we must be bold, if we would be strong.

Thus is it in regard to spiritual things. We must act as Christians, believing that we are such, or we can accomplish very little. It is a miserable abuse of life, opposed to all efficiency and usefulness, to be forever doubting and weighing evidences, and balancing for years between hope and fear, not daring to assume the responsibilities and do the work of Christians, for fear of being deceived. It cannot be that God intends that one should live thus. I will admit all you may say concerning our frailty, and the deceitfulness of an evil heart, but I cannot admit that there is no deliverance from the danger, or that God will leave any one, who honestly seeks light and trusts Him for it, to delusion and the believing of a lie.

Doubtless the degree of evidence will vary. There have been those who have had such revelations through the Spirit, such conscious fellowship with God, that they have said that it was impossible for them to doubt; yes, some have grown very bold, and affirmed that they were as certain of their acceptance with God as of their existence.

I do not say that all are to be expected to use such language. With those of a naturally diffident temper it would be an impossibility. But all may certainly reach a position of firm, satisfying persuasion; not of hope merely, far more—of settled confidence, excluding fear, excluding doubt.

Why not? Paul so attained. Do you say, He had visions and revelations for his encouragement? But he did not rely on such evidences. He seldom referred to them. Fourteen years passed after he was "caught up into heaven" before he spoke of it; and when he did so, in order to vindicate his assailed apostleship, he apologized for it, saying, "I am become a fool in glorying, but ye have compelled me."

No, it was not on signs and wonders that his *confidence was built, but on those promises* and provisions of grace in which all have a common share. Why, then, may we not attain the same persuasion?

Before giving a full answer to this question, let us look more carefully at *the foundation on which the confidence expressed in the text was based.* We shall find it to be simply the character and power of the Redeemer. Many seem to think that when one expresses any degree of assurance it must be from a feeling of self-satisfaction, and that he must look at his heart and life with much complacency.

Now nothing could be more opposed to the apostle's way of thinking than such a spirit. He was as far as possible from justifying himself, or professing to be content with his spiritual attainments. He abhorred the thought of being his own saviour. Let him speak for himself. "I know that in me, that is in my flesh, dwelleth no good thing." "Not as though I had already attained, either were already perfect." "I count not myself to have apprehended; but this one thing I do, forgetting those things which are behind, and reaching forth unto those things which are before, I press toward the mark for the prize of the high calling of God in Christ Jesus." These were the words of a man by no means satisfied with his own righteousness; plainly conscious of remaining sin. And there has been noticed a striking gradation in his expressions of self-disparagement. At first he called himself "the least of the apostles"; after five more years of growth in grace, he was "less than the least of all saints"; but at the end of his Christian course, he could not speak even of sinners, without adding, "of whom I am chief."

Yet this man was hopeful — was confident. Standing on the verge of the grave, he could look up through the dungeon's gloom and say, "Henceforth there is laid up for me a crown of righteousness, which the Lord, the righteous judge, shall give me at that day."

We ask for the grounds of this exultant expectation; and the reply comes in the words before us, "I know whom I have believed." He looked constantly away from, and above himself. He felt that his soul was not safe in his own keeping, and so committed it to another, giving Him the charge of defending its interests, pleading its cause, securing its pardon. As one whose honor is assailed or property imperilled, looks to his advocate to protect his name, and rescue his estate in court; so had Paul become the client of the great Advocate before the bar of God. And he knew that interests committed to such guardianship were safe against all the world; safe against all the powers of hell.

Two things are required in any one undertaking such a charge, in order that we may rest fearlessly upon him; fidelity and power. We must be assured that he will be mindful of our cause, and do for us all he can; and then that he is able to secure our deliverance.

Can we doubt that when, conscious of our own helplessness, we have committed our souls to the Saviour, He will be faithful to the trust? I cannot set myself to argue the trust-worthiness of our Lord Jesus Christ. His name forbids a doubt or fear. What associations cluster around it. The very object of His advent was "to seek and to save that which was lost." "Though He was rich, yet for our sakes He became poor, that we through His poverty might be rich." "He laid down His life for us." What stronger proof could He give of His desire to save? Remember the feelings towards sinners which He manifested daily by word and deed. What crowds followed Him; and how did He ever stand amid this throng of the helpless and despairing, with hands outstretched, and countenance benign. From what suppliant did He ever turn away? When the end of His course was drawing nigh, we hear Him exulting before His Father: "Those that Thou gavest me I have kept, and none of them is lost."

Can we fear, then, to trust Him? He undertakes our cause, not reluctantly prevailed on by entreaties, not purchased by a fee; scorn, and pain, and death was what man paid Him; but He, himself, loved and longed for our souls, and is anxious now to deliver us. "How often would I," He exclaims even to those unwilling to accept His grace, "but ye would not."

If, then, His fidelity to the trust is certain, can we doubt His power? Listen. "All power is given unto me, in Heaven and on earth." "Thou hast given Him power over all flesh, that He should give eternal life to as many as thou hast given Him." "They shall never perish, neither shall any man pluck them out of my hand." "I am He that hath the keys of hell and death,"—"that openeth, and no man shutteth, and shutteth and no man openeth." While manifest on earth, He said, "Thy sins are forgiven, go in peace"; and when they questioned His authority to say this, He wrought a miracle to prove that He had a Divine right to pardon sin.

Such is that Saviour, to whom the apostle committed his soul; to whom we commit ours. He has lost none of His attributes; nay He is now exalted, that He may complete this work of delivering sinners. He died for them, and His recompence is, to receive them when they turn in penitence, to wash them from their sins in His blood, and welcome them to Heaven. Must we not be safe, with such a helper? How fitting the jubilant cry, "I know whom I have believed; I am persuaded that He is able to keep that which I have committed unto Him against that day." While Paul had before him the vision of that all-sufficient Redeemer, how could he doubt?

We return to the question, *Why may not we exercise the same faith, and rejoice in the same assurance?* Has Christ changed; His love grown cold; His power been exhausted? Has He relinquished the charge of perishing souls? Whence, then, all these misgivings?

Perhaps the old difficulty comes up again: "We are so unworthy." But is it not evident that this pretext has no pertinence whatever? Acceptance rests on a different ground. If a king should meet a beggar in rags, and call him to the hall of audience, would that beggar have any right to say, "I cannot go, for my clothing is unfit?" What has he to do with his appearance, if the king, seeing what it was, nevertheless called him? Would it not be pride; would it not be contempt of majesty for him to be thinking more of his rags, than of the gracious invitation? Let him go, just as he is: he may, perchance, come forth arrayed in fairer apparel.

So, when the sinner is called to go to Jesus, with all his weakness and all his guilt, is it for him to dwell only on his unfitness, and hesitate and fear? Did not Christ know all, when He called him? If He is willing to receive the outcast, and cover his vileness with His own spotless robe, shall the favor be refused?

Would that you might see that under the distrust so often expressed, and so often, I fear, cherished as akin to a becoming humility, there is lurking pride, a subtle thought that our acceptance in some measure depends on our own goodness, and a contempt for offered grace. We seem to be disparaging ourselves, when in truth we are wronging Him who seeks to save us.

Oh, there would be far fewer misgivings, and far more confidence, if we could only have such low views of ourselves, that we should entirely forget ourselves, and see only that Saviour, through whom the ungodly are justified. Could we but see Him as he is, and hear His voice, so gentle, so loving; could we but heartily believe in the blessed freeness and fulness of His grace; could we but understand what it is really and entirely to commit the soul to Him; how when that is done, all is done; how He takes the soul with all its guilt, to justify and cleanse it by His mighty power; could we but be willing to let Him have the whole glory of our salvation, not even thinking of obtaining any for ourselves in any way; then should we come far nearer than we do to the blessed simplicity of the truth in Jesus, and find strong consolation, and ever-shining hope. Losing ourselves, we should be found in Christ. Giving up all for Him, we should possess all in Him.

In concluding, I wish to press these truths upon the attention, especially, of two classes found in every congregation.

First, those who have long been under religious impressions, but are still undecided. They are not easy in sin; they have desires, real though perhaps faint, to be Christians: sometimes they have hoped they were; but nothing is fixed — nothing definite. Time passes, possibly year after year, and when they ought to be growing strong in the Lord, they are still as babes.

The other class is that larger one of professed followers of Christ, who hope tremblingly, doubtfully. They have no real religious enjoyment; they dare not speak confidently; they dare not venture on those duties — of teaching and exhortation, for example — which require one to feel satisfied as to his own state. They have long lived so, and there is a prospect of their dying so, unless, as perhaps they hope, some special grace overtake them at the last hour.

My heart is heavy as I speak these words. Not to have such distressed inquirers, such timid disciples, did Christ die. The Gospel can do more than this for sinners; it is "glad tidings of great joy." It has its stern doctrines and severe reproofs, which we may not hide; but grace — grace is its characteristic. If we forget this, we pervert the truth, and do injustice to a merciful God.

You may have read an account, recently published, of the last hours of an eminent divine, Dr. Spring, of Newbury. Said he to a ministerial brother, "I have finished my work; I have tried to preach the Gospel; I have been instrumental in establishing the seminary at Andover; and now the question is, Has my motive been right? If it has, I shall receive my reward; if not, I shall lose it. I hardly know what to believe about myself. But it matters not. We are but atoms, and it is of little consequence what becomes of us. God will be glorified in the result, whatever it may be."

We must feel the sublimity of such a state of self-abnegation and supreme desire that God should rule. But did not that holy man — for he was a holy man — fail somewhat in his views of the sufficiency of Christ? Was he not scrutinizing his motives, as if he were to enter heaven by his own righteousness, when it would have been better for him to have taken all his imperfections and sins and cast them, as a load too heavy for himself to bear, at the Saviour's feet, relying, in sweet and unquestioning confidence, on the plenteousness of His grace? Forgive me for seeming to censure one truly worthy of veneration, but I must say it, a believer, with the Gospel in his hands, ought not so to have died. That sovereign God, before whom he abased himself so humbly, was not anxious to condemn, but to save. He was a God of mercy.

Thus would I have you regard these doubts, not as necessary and becoming signs of humility, but as blemishes in the Christian character. "The blood of Jesus Christ cleanseth from all sin," so that not a spot remains. The robe of His righteousness can cover the vilest offender; and in Him we are wholly to trust.

We can see now more than ever how much significance there was in Christ's eating and drinking with publicans and sinners. It shocked the Pharisees; but He meant to show to all ages that sinners were welcome to approach Him. For the same reason, He suffered a polluted woman to touch His pure body. The natural Pharisaism of the human heart still objects to such approaches; it talks of being fit to go to Jesus, not knowing that

> "All the fitness He requires,
> Is to feel our need of Him,"

and to have love for Him in our hearts.

Here let me say that real love may exist, even while there is remaining sin. Some suppose that while we offend we never can be sure that we love.

But may not a man be truly, even devotedly, attached to his wife, who, nevertheless, at times selfishly disregards her wishes, speaks angry words that have a cut and sting in them, and bring tears to the eye? Yet down beneath all these occasional excitements are depths of pure, unalterable affection. So may one truly love Christ, though because of the waywardness of a nature only partially sanctified, and the pressure of temptation, he may be at times unfaithful to that love. Peter was a true disciple, yet he denied his Lord.

Therefore, in judging of his state, one is not to look only at his offences as evidences against himself, but is permitted to ask, Have I not reason to think, notwithstanding all my inconsistencies, that I do love Christ, and am loved by Him? Finding such evidence, he is to cleave to his Saviour, venture on His grace, go forth boldly in His service, and, looking away from himself, to exclaim in the confidence of faith, "I know whom I have believed."

Do we not need more of this spirit? Ye who are halting and undecided, ye who are tossed between hope and fear are wronging your own souls. You are depriving yourselves of attainable joy and strength; you are famishing in the very presence of the full table of God.

We desire no self-complacency, nor to have any feel that they have attained; but would it not be like a sun rising on our darkness, if more could stand up and say, We have gained such views of the sufficiency of Christ that all our fears are gone. Never did we more plainly see our sinfulness nor loathe it more; but through the Gospel we have lost our dread of its condemning power; unworthy as we are, we look confidently for salvation through Him who loved us and gave Himself for us; we shrink not from the conflicts of life nor the darkness of the valley of death, for neither life nor death shall separate us from His love.

Then with what cheerfulness and ardor should we speak of Christ, and labor for Christ, till the unbelieving felt it, and believed also. Our firmness of faith would give us access to all hearts. This activity then, would, by its reflex influence, keep our fears still further away. When Dr. Marshman, the missionary, was a young man, his mind was often darkened. After thirty years of labor in India he returned to England, and William Jay said to him, "Well, Doctor, how about those doubts and fears?" "Haven't had time for them," was the reply. If Christians here would be more active for their Master, under the impulse of a heartier faith, would not they also find less time for the gloomy thoughts which now oppress them?

Shall we not seek a more confident and comforting trust? Believing that "God is love," clasping to our hearts the Gospel, with its "exceeding great and precious promises," looking unto Jesus, "the author and finisher of our faith," let us press forward, saying ever:

"I stand on Zion's mount,
And view my starry crown;
No power on earth my hope can shake,
Nor hell can thrust me down.

The vaulted heavens shall fall,
Built by Jehovah's hands;
But firmer than the heavens, the Rock
Of my salvation stands."

Persistency of Piety.

CAST THY BREAD UPON THE WATERS; FOR THOU SHALT FIND IT AFTER MANY DAYS. *Ecclesiastes,* xi.: 1.

WHEN the river has overflowed its banks and deposited upon the broad fields on either side its fertilizing slime, the Oriental rice-sower scatters his seed. It will grow better, we are told, if deposited before the inundation has subsided, that is, literally "cast upon the waters"; then, ere long, he may hope to see it springing up luxuriantly, and in due season to receive a plentiful return.

The text does not contain a maxim for husbandmen, but applies their experience to our spiritual concerns. In these we are to act in faith; to labor when there seems as little promise of any return as when the water receives and hides the scattered seed, and we shall find our recompense in the end. It may not be at once; probably it will not be; yet the blessing shall come "after many days." We must expect often to wait, must be willing to wait, and we shall receive it at last.

Thus viewed, this Scripture is a warning against impatience — against the thought we are so prone to indulge, that we are accomplishing nothing unless we can see the immediate results.

That we may take this warning, let us consider, First, *how slowly God often moves in the accomplishment of His designs.* He is never in haste. Why should He be? What is time to Him? "A thousand years in Thy sight are but as yesterday when it is past, and as a watch in the night."

There are two causes of impatience with us, which do not affect God. One is our inability to see what is future. We are like those looking at a curtain dropped — our vision limited. The result must appear, become actual, or we cannot be sure of it. But God "seeth the end from the beginning," and rejoices in results ages before they are discerned by human eyes.

Again, we have the conviction that what we do, must be done at once, or not at all. Life is short, and quickly fleeting. But who shall measure — who shall limit the lifetime of God?

Therefore He lays out plans on a vast scale, extending over continents, requiring the coöperation of successive generations. He gives a promise, and waits till "the fulness of time" comes for its accomplishment. The changes of nature, and the events of human life occur in accordance with His designs; but His purposes concerning them were eternal, and He is contented with the gradual evolution of those purposes.

Let us look at one or two familiar illustrations of this. Man began to exist about six thousand years ago; the earth was furnished for his use; he was intended to be, as he is, the head of this terrestrial creation. Now a human artificer, if we may suppose him to have laid the foundations of the earth, would have been eager to have completed the creation without delay. The world would have appeared to him intolerably desolate and solitary until there existed here those capable of the intelligent enjoyment and use of the things which were made.

Was it so with God? We have abundant evidence that it was not. Thousands of years passed — no one can say how many thousands — and the earth was preparing, by convulsions, by the growth and destruction of gigantic plants, and their consolidation into enormous beds of coal, by the submerging of continents, and the upheaval of mountain ridges: was thus preparing, age by age, to be the world it is to-day, a full treasure-house of metal and mineral; its climate regulated in part by these mountain chains, made for that service; its surface diversified, adapted for various productions, and to sustain races with different habits and customs.

The process might have been hastened; and if any ask, Why did not the Almighty put forth the full energies of His omnipotence, and accomplish these results more quickly? the answer to be given is the same with which we may check ourselves in regard to the Providential mysteries of to-day: "My thoughts are not your thoughts, neither are your ways My ways, saith the Lord."

Still more strange appears the slow unfolding of Divine truth and mercy in the redemption of the world. It must ever remain a mystery to us why so long a period elapsed, after the plan was formed and announced, before its execution; why the patriarchs and righteous men of old saw only in types and shadows Him, who might even then have appeared; why so many nations lived and died in total ignorance of His coming; why, after His advent, the Spirit, who like a rushing wind shook the house at Jerusalem, and the hearts of three thousand at once, did not sweep round the circuit of the world, converting all tribes of men before that first age had passed; why Omnipotence has been restrained and Grace limited, and the cause of salvation made slow progress even to our day.

It is not merely because men have been unfaithful, for God himself, with reverence we say it, has not exerted all His power, nor made the fullest possible manifestation of His saving mercy. He has done all that was best, certainly far more than we deserved; still His power has been restrained. Holding fast to His purpose that the world shall be filled with His glory, rejoicing over the salvation of men and desiring the death of none, He has yet suffered His cause to advance slowly. He has often removed those who seemed to be effecting most good, and given strange success to the schemes of their enemies. As of old He waited ages before He created man, so is He waiting other ages for the recovery of the race from ruin.

Let us observe, Secondly, that as God himself thus waits for the slow accomplishment of His designs, *He often, by the arrangements of His Providence, compels men to be contented with a gradual progress and success.* In our ordinary enterprises we are continually restrained, our plans and wishes ever outrunning our capacity of execution.

What a check upon us, for example, is the necessity of resting after a few hours of bodily or mental toil. How much more could we accomplish, were it not that one third part of our existence must be given up to slumber. Napoleon Bonaparte showed us what a sleepless man can do. When environed by dangers, he repeatedly passed successive days and nights dictating to several secretaries at once. Letters, bulletins, dispatches, poured from his cabinet, like the flakes of the snow-storm; all Europe was filled by his terrible presence, and trembled.

Then the execution of our plans generally depends in part upon others, and thus obstacles and delays arise. The sickness, detention, treachery of one keeps back many, and they lose all their labor. We must confide often in another's judgment, and are liable to be baffled by his mistakes. Death suddenly takes away one on whom we were depending, and his knowledge and experience perish with him.

Seldom, in a word, is it possible for one to march by a straight and short path to the goal of his desires. Is he aiming at wealth, or office, or re-renown? It is only after reverses, and hope long deferred, and many labors and anxieties that he can obtain what he is seeking. Others will never know by how many secret efforts he has advanced to the attainment of his aims; how long that success he seems to have easily won has been the object of his constant aspirations, and of endeavors hidden from the sight of all.

Thus has it been so arranged by God, that in this world success must cost labor, anxiety, perseverance, patience, indomitable will. He who sets his heart on immediate enjoyment will be disappointed, like the husbandman who should expect the harvest just after he has planted. He must cast forth his seed, and he shall find it "after many days."

We would now remark, Thirdly, that *this law of delay applies to spiritual things:* to our efforts to advance, in ourselves and among others, the cause of piety.

Take, as one illustration, *the work of preaching.* This is God's ordinance. He promises to bless it. "My word shall not return unto me void," He says. But how seldom do we see any immediate result. The truth falls, according to our Saviour's comparison, like seed into the ground, and, like the seed, it may be long in springing up. One may receive it even unconsciously. A remark may enter the mind, and the memory store it away unperceived. It vanishes from sight, it would seem to have been forgotten, but in the secret chambers of the mind it is kept till its hour comes, and then it reappears, a thought, barbed like the arrow to convict, or soft as the sweet music of the harp to soothe and cheer.

Years may thus pass, ere the effect is produced. So was it with a sermon of the godly Flavel. His text was that solemn adjuration, "If any man love not the Lord Jesus Christ, let him be anathema." As, at the close of the services, he rose to pronounce the benediction, he hesitated and exclaimed, "How can I bless those whom God hath pronounced accursed?" A young man, about twenty years of age, heard and turned away unmoved. He emigrated to America; he settled in a town in Massachusetts; God spared him in his sin until his hundredth birthday. On that day his thoughts went back to the scenes of his youth. He saw the faithful preacher again, heard the words uttered eighty years before, and was overwhelmed at the thought that during that whole century of an impenitent life, the curse of God had been resting upon him. The seed was found at last, and it bore fruit to eternal life.

Therefore, the preacher is to labor in confidence, and to hope on even when no bright tokens of success meet the eye. He serves One who forgets not His promise, though its fulfilment may be delayed.

Another example of the operation of this law may be found in *the effects of parental instruction.* Essential as this is, it is often discouraging. "Line must be upon line, and precept upon precept." It is a work of endless repetitions; it is never done. When some impression seems to have been made, some habit to have been broken, some imperious temper to have been subdued, just when we are congratulating ourselves upon success, the old evil starts up, vigorous as ever. I have heard of breaking the will "once for all." It is a beautiful theory; but I have known of wills broken fifty times at least, and having life in them still. And so many a discouraged parent says that his labor has been in vain.

But it is not so. Despite these failures, he is wielding a mighty power. He is gradually attaining his end. One partial and temporary triumph over evil is preparing the way for a more decisive victory. His words are not all forgotten; they are being laid by for the future. The tremulous accents of a voice quivering with emotion in prayer, entreaty, admonition, the soft pressure of a loving hand, may make impressions which will be remembered when that voice is silent and that hand is cold. The impalpable, indescribable power of parental love and life may be moulding the character with resistless force, though the progress can no more be measured than the daily growth of a tree, advancing by imperceptible changes to its beautiful blossoming and prolific fruitage.

The same principle regulates *the influence of seasons and occasions of prayer.* This also is an appointment of God. When we call, He promises to hear. But He has never pledged immediate answers. Some petitions, like those for deliverance from imminent peril, must be answered at once, if at all; and then, while men are speaking God doth hear. But most supplications admit of delay; they are heard, are remembered; they are "as a memorial before God"; it is determined that the favor sought shall be granted, but in the time and the way God sees best; and while the impatient and distrustful suppliants are complaining that their breath is spent in vain, He is preparing to do exceeding abundantly for them, beyond their utmost thoughts.

There are instances on record in which Christians have made one request the burden of their daily prayer for successive years, and though their faith was tried, the reward of their unfainting perseverance came at last.

So as to the benefit resulting from seasons of social prayer. There is a disposition with some always to judge of this by the emotions excited at the time; especially, to make the degree of enjoyment felt the exponent of the good resulting. But some other emotion may at certain times be more fitting than exultation, and the graciousness of God appear in humbling those who need to be brought low; in making those dissatisfied who are to be roused to fresh consecration and activity.

John Newton was narrating the experience of many besides himself when he wrote:

"I asked the Lord that I might grow
In faith, and love, and every grace;
Might more of His salvation know,
And seek more earnestly His face.

"'T was He who taught me thus to pray,
And He, I trust, has answered prayer;
But it has been in such a way,
As almost drove me to despair."

Now, as the individual is to pray on, though immediate encouragements are withheld, is not the Church also to be persistent and importunate, waiting, yet looking ever to the Lord? As the clouds sometimes hold the water for a long time, while the parched earth lies thirsty beneath them, so do clouds of blessing gather, and months pass by before they break in gladdening streams. We are to trust God; and to think that no benefit follows our prayers and meetings which is not striking and apparent, argues more zeal than knowledge, more fervor than faith.

One more illustration in this connection must be presented. It is afforded by *the judgments passed concerning what are called "the means of conversion."* When one has been brought to a knowledge of the truth, reference is too often made to the immediate agency in the awakening, while other accompanying influences are left out of sight. For example, it is said that such a sermon, or reproof, or a particular affliction, or such a book, was the instrument of the conversion of the soul. Yet this is but part of the truth. That instrument accomplished its work only because other agencies had been operating before.

Behold a flinty rock. A hundred workmen are ranged in order, to break it. The first heaves high his ponderous hammer and strikes; it rings upon the stone and sparks of fire fly out, but the stone seems unaffected. The second, the third, do the same with the same result. After a while a crack appears; probably it was not discovered at its first existence. The fissure widens under successive blows, till at last the hundredth man, weaker than the rest, lifts his hammer, and the rock parts. Did he do the work? The broken mass fell beneath his arm, but is it the truth to say that he broke it?

Now, what is spoken of as the means of conversion, is often only this hundredth blow. No one but God can tell how many and what agencies are efficient, by His blessing and coöperation, in saving men. The prayers and instructions of parents; the words of Scripture, of tracts, of memoirs, perhaps of newspapers; words dropped accidentally, as we say, in conversation; the voice of public worship and preaching; joys, bereavements, losses; some scene of piety in humble life; the sad end of some bold transgressor; all, all the events, and voices, and ministries of life God patiently uses; and the momentous change, which in its real occurrence is instantaneous, may have been prepared for through long successive years. Many have contributed to it who "cast their seed upon the waters" and "find it after many days."

Thus, in all these instances, God has so arranged events that results shall not follow efforts in quick and rapid succession, but after a season of delay. So He would train men to be patient like Himself, waiting in confidence for the gradual accomplishment of their plans.

We are led, then, as the proper conclusion of our theme, to this lesson: that *in doing good, in serving God, in striving to advance His cause, we are to be calm, resolute, persevering, walking not by sight but faith.* We are to be men who, through good report and evil report, amid circumstances discouraging as well as animating, will hold on our steady way:

> "Like the star, unhasting;
> Like the star, unresting."

Do not let me seem to be discouraging zeal: I am pleading for zeal of the highest and most effective character; not fed by impulsive emotion, but drawing life from the most fixed determination.

The character of the present Emperor of the French is well known. He is not excitable, his countenance never glows with emotion, he never acts precipitately; but beneath that smooth, cold surface are depths of resistless purpose. For many years, when an exile and a prisoner, he kept his eyes on the throne of France, predicting, when all laughed at him, his present elevation. And now he holds the sceptre with the tightest grasp, and executes his inflexible will. Remonstrances, threatenings are lost upon him. Always he appears to the public the same impassive, iron man; and opposition is awed by that calmness more than by the most fierce and noisy resistance.

I speak of this to show that quietness may consist with strength; that a Christian may be thoroughly earnest, yet calm. I would not recommend such an unmoved exterior — it is unnatural; but would that we might have the same tenacity of purpose and superiority to discouragements. We are to pray, and preach, and struggle against sin; we are to hold up the standard of the Church at home, and go forth to meet her foes, with an unwavering purpose and hope. Never are we to check our desires for any good, but to have desires so strong that we shall be willing to labor, and labor on, though we see no immediate results.

Because we have warned a child faithfully, or spoken once to an impenitent friend or Sabbath School scholar, apparently in vain, we are not to abandon the effort. Because the Church is not revived as we desire, we are not to say that God has forsaken us. Because we cannot see what we are accomplishing by efforts which we believe to be in accordance with God's will, we are not to give them up. "Behold, the husbandman waiteth for the precious fruit of the earth, and hath long patience for it, until he receive the early and the latter rain. Be ye also patient, and stablish your hearts."

It seems to be a law, that what is to endure long shall be long in reaching perfection. A few hours from the birth of an insect it rejoices in the full maturity of its powers; but in a day or two it perishes. Man's lifetime is seventy years, and through twenty of them he is immature. He can bide his time, for, comparatively, he has long to live. And shall not we be willing to toil on for many years, helping forward a work so great and lasting as this of the salvation of the immortal soul, and the establishment of Christ's unchanging kingdom? We may die; but that soul, for which we have yearned, will still live. We may die; but the influence of the Church, for which we have prayed, and which, by our connection with it, has been strengthened, will bless succeeding times. What repetition of endeavor, what prolonged perseverance should we grudge, when such high ends are to be attained?

If the law of the universe were, that cause and effect should always be linked in direct sequence, we might at times despond; but since God delays His grandest works, since He retards man in almost all his movements, even as He places an interval between the sowing and the ripening of the seed, what so befits us as a resolute, believing steadiness in every religious work?

We know, by the word of God, that if we abound in such labors they shall not be in vain. The promise is to gladden us when we see no visible encouragement. Said one to Dr. Judson, "How bright appear to you the prospects of the world's conversion?" "Just as bright as the promises of God," was the noble reply.

Therefore, "cast your seed upon the waters." Scatter it broadcast in the family, in the Church, in all places of your social intercourse and of your business activity, by word, by gift, by deed. Despond not though it disappear from sight; for the word is as sure as though it blazed on the firmament in letters of stars: "Thou shall find it after many days."

The Book of Psalms.

David, the son of Jesse, said, and the man who was raised up on high, the anointed of the God of Jacob, and the sweet psalmist of Israel, said: The Spirit of the Lord spake by me, and His Word was in my tongue. II. *Samuel*, xxiii.: 1—2.

AMONG the canonical Scriptures which have come to us with undisputed authority, honored by the Jews, always reverently spoken of by the Messiah, and held in equal esteem by all bodies of Christians, is the Book of Psalms. This book is unlike all others in the Bible in its style, structure, and uses. It is a book of poetry, written by various authors, at different times, conveying practical instruction and doctrine in the form of sacred lyrics, for the most part adapted to the purposes of public worship.

Of these songs of praise, the son of Jesse, who is so truly spoken of as "as a man raised on high," "the sweet Psalmist of Israel," was the principal author. Seventy-three, mostly in the first part of the book, are expressly ascribed to him, and he doubtless composed several of those which are anonymous; others have a later, and a few an earlier origin. The ninetieth Psalm is designated, in accordance with a most ancient tradition, "the prayer of Moses"; others were written by Asaph, by the sons of Korah, and one, or, as some think, two, by Solomon. These all breathe a common sentiment; and we do not doubt that all the composers could say as David did, "the Spirit of the Lord spake by me, and His Word was in my tongue." The collection was probably arranged in its present form by Ezra, about four hundred and fifty years before Christ.

But the point of special interest to us in regard to this book is, *What are its present uses?* Why was such a collection of sacred poems included in the Scriptures?

In the First place, we ought not to forget *the literary beauty of these Hebrew songs.* The Scriptures do far more, indeed, than minister to a cultivated taste, yet we are not to despise the Divine wisdom, which has seen fit to communicate truth in a form to commend it to the scholar as well as the peasant. He who adapted the world to the eye which seeks for the beautiful and sublime, with the same kindness made the Bible attractive to the sensitive and cultured mind, "a volume of heavenly doctrine, but withal of earthly adaptation." Nor can we fail to regard it as in some measure a triumph for the truth, that many who have shown themselves averse to the morals of the book, have been constrained to do homage to its grandeur, and though they have disregarded its teachings, have yet confessed, to their own condemnation, that it was Divine.

The Psalms, we have said, are in the garb of poetry. They do not indeed flow in measured numbers, nor in rhyme. Such is not the structure of Hebrew verse. It is mainly distinguished by a kind of correspondence, or parallelism, between the clauses of each stanza: a double repetition of the same idea.

The style of composition, also, which we can judge of better than the form of the verse, is highly poetic. It is elevated, stately, living, and dramatic: full of pathos and sublimity. To a remarkable degree it is metaphorical. The good man, for example, as we read of him in the first Psalm, is not described by his qualities; he is "like a tree planted by the rivers of water, that bringeth forth his fruit in his season." So the doctrine that God will guard and supply us is not stated abstractly;

but he moves before us a "Shepherd," who leadeth His flock "in green pastures, and beside the still waters." Again, in the eighteenth Psalm, it is not formally declared that God's people were in distress, but He is entreated to look down upon "the vine," which He brought from Egypt, and planted, and caused to fill the land, till the hills were covered with its shadow, and its boughs were like goodly cedars; but which had been broken down, so that they which passed by plucked it, and the wild beast devoured it.

The objects of nature, also, are depicted in the most vivid manner. The twenty-ninth Psalm is the description of a thunder storm, coming up over the Mediterranean. "The voice of the Lord is upon the waters, powerful and full of majesty." The storm rolls on over Lebanon; "the voice of the Lord breaketh the cedars." It still advances; "the Lord shaketh the wilderness of Kadesh."

Equally graphic is the one hundred and fourth Psalm, which Humboldt speaks of as presenting a picture of the entire Cosmos; adding, "We are astonished to see within the compass of a poem so brief, the universe, the heavens, and the earth, drawn with a few grand strokes."

The poet Milman says: "In comparison with the hymns of David, the sacred poetry of all other nations sinks into insignificance." Campbell, also, pays a similar tribute to the beauty of these songs; adding, "The most inspired aspect of David's mind presents itself when he looks abroad on the universe with the eye of a poet, and the heart of a glad and grateful worshipper. When he looks up to the starry firmament, his soul assimilates to its splendor and serenity." Then, speaking of the same psalm which Humboldt so greatly admired, he declares: "The impression of that exquisite ode dilates the heart with a pleasure too instinctive and simple to be described."

It is true that all this is not necessarily homage to David's Lord; there is no essential piety in such emotions of pleasure. Yet, we may be thankful that God has invested His Word with such charms; and now, when the crowd of conceited scoffers is increasing, and when the Old Testament is sneered at as obsolete, we are glad to meet these free thinkers with the challenge to show us in the writings they most delight in, anything loftier or more beautiful than God has given us in the Bible; to meet the student, venerating the ancient strains of the "Father of Poetry," and say, a greater than Homer is here; lo, here is a sacred ode which was sung six hundred years before he was born.

We would ask the unbeliever, also, to explain how it has happened that, among a race in many respects unpolished and unlearned, there arose bards surpassing, in the elevation and breadth of their vision, and in the clear, pure dignity of their hymns of praise, all that ever came from nations renowned for wonders of art, and the highest achievements of philosophy and eloquence. How can this be accounted for, save by recognizing an inspiration from above?

Let me remind you, Secondly, that the Psalms are to be prized for *their doctrinal teachings.* Where else do we find such views of the perfection of God? Very many of these songs are devoted to the rehearsing of His attributes. What reverence, and humble adoration, and grateful praise breathe through them all. How generally they end with God, with whatever they begin. How are not only men, but everything which hath breath, and even inanimate things, "snow and vapors, mountains and all hills, fruitful trees and all cedars," called on to praise Jehovah?

Take, as a single illustration, the description of Divine Omniscience and Omnipresence in the one hundred and thirty-ninth Psalm: "O Lord, Thou hast searched me and known me. Whither shall I go from Thy Spirit, or whither shall I flee from Thy presence?" Then the poor wanderer, hiding from God, is tracked to every quarter of the univ^rse, to heaven, to hell, to the uttermost parts of the sea, and everywhere God is found, seeing and holding him. Even the darkness doth not cover him, but "the night shineth as the day." Can you conceive of a representation of these attributes more impressive or complete?

With equal fidelity do the Psalms portray the character of man; the uncertainty and vanity of his life; above all, his moral frailty and guilt. Not a few of them are penitential; and where, in all the unveilings of the heart's inmost depths, do you find such acknowledgments of the hatefulness of sin, or self-condemnation more full and unsparing? The fifty-first Psalm has never had its parallel among all the ejaculations of the heart-broken. There sin shows out the very secret of its vileness, as committed against God: "Against Thee, Thee only, have I sinned." There depravity is traced to its source in hereditary corruption: "behold, I was shapen in iniquity." And there, too, even there, shines amid the darkness the hope of mercy: "a broken and a contrite heart, O Lord, Thou wilt not despise."

Other Psalms, like the fifty-eighth, set forth the guilt of transgressors without equivocation or disguise; and show impending over them the avenging arm of a justly indignant God. Those which are styled "imprecatory," are sublimely instructive on this same point of the inherent evil of sin. They are not effusions of personal vindictiveness, but the protests of a soul stirred to its depths against stout-hearted and defiant offenders. They are cries for just vengeance, such as Milton expressed in his sonnet,

> "Avenge, O Lord, thy slaughtered saints, whose bones
> Lie scattered on the Alpine mountains cold; —"

and such as go up now from pure hearts in view of audacious iniquity; God's voice of equity in the breast, which cannot keep silence, which need not always be suppressed.

Here, also, we have glimpses of that truth which was to be the centre and the sum of the new revelation, — Christ, the incarnate, the suffering, the conqueror. Who can forget that He said: "All things must be fulfilled, which are written in the Psalms concerning me"? Forty-eight passages from this book are quoted in the New Testament. David, like Abraham, rejoiced to see Christ's day by faith. He testified through the Spirit, in the second Psalm, of His Divine Sonship. In the twenty-second, he anticipated His cries amid sorrows and reproaches: "I am poured out like water; all my bones are out of joint; the assembly of the wicked have enclosed me; they pierced my hands and my feet." "My God, my God, why hast thou forsaken me?"

At other times brighter visions rise, and the harp of the psalmist is swept to joyful strains: "My heart is inditing a good matter: Thou art fairer than the children of men; Thy throne, O God, is for ever and ever." Then, again, the future triumph of the Church is disclosed: "God is the king of all the earth; God reigneth over the heathen." The sublime, and as yet unfulfilled, conception is given of One who shall rule with perfect justice, the sceptre of whose kingdom is "a right sceptre"; whose dominion shall extend "to the ends of the earth"; who "shall spare the poor and the needy"; whose glory shall fill the earth, and whose name, with consenting voice, all nations shall bless.

"O scenes surpassing fable, and yet true!"

How has this mourning earth been waiting amid the struggles of selfishness and pride, and the ceaseless inhumanity of man to man, for this glorious empire of Right — of universal Fraternity and universal Peace.

We think of these varied truths, which are brought before us in this book, and of the climax of all in the revelation of the person and triumphs of Christ, and heartily say with Bishop Horne, "This little volume, like the paradise of Eden, affords us in perfection every thing that groweth elsewhere, every tree pleasant to the sight and good for food; and above all, what was there lost but is here restored, *the tree of life in the midst of the garden.*"

But the chief and peculiar use of the Psalms has not yet been considered. Let us notice, in the Third place, *their devotional character.* It is an instinct of the pious soul to worship; a necessity for the heart overcharged with emotion to pour out its full tribute of praise. Here is a model for us in all such exercises; a heaven-built pathway, on which our thoughts and desires may travel upward. When we would know how to approach our God, what pleas to urge, what boons to crave; when our invention fails to give us fitting language to set forth His glory or express our need, we have here an inspired liturgy, rich in its variety of topic, expressing every mood of the changing feelings, and bearing us, as on eagle's wings, up to the throne of God.

Wonderfully was David prepared by a most diversified experience to enter into and express the emotions of men of every condition. The sheep pastures, the camp, the palace, the temple, all contributed to his training. He walked on the high places of prosperity, yet knew the keenest of human woes. He was the friend of God, yet was suffered to fall into most debasing sin, and compelled to struggle back through the rough paths of bereavement and penitence. His words, therefore, wake an echo in the hearts of all; his songs enter into the religious life of the whole world.

I wish to show by some quotations how Christians have prized them; yet out of the crowd of waiting witnesses, I know not which to select. Shall we hear Augustine, speaking from the fourth century? "O, what accents did I utter unto Thee in those Psalms, and how was I by them kindled towards Thee and on fire to rehearse them through the whole world, as a protest against the pride of mankind. How I would they had been near me when I read the fourth Psalm, in that time of my rest: 'Hear me when I call, O God of my righteousness.' I trembled for fear, and again kindled with hope, and with rejoicing in Thy mercy."

Luther also drew from this book no small portion of his courage. He hung favorite extracts from it around the walls of his chamber. And he asks, in the confidence of one speaking from experience, and with that poetic sensitiveness which adorned his rugged nature, like flowers growing from the cleft rock, "Where do we find a sweeter voice of joy than in these songs of praise? There you look into the heart of the godly, as into a garden, as into Paradise itself. What sweet blossoms are there unfolding of all glad thoughts towards God and His goodness. The Psalter forms a little book for all saints, in which each shall find sentiments applicable to his own case, so expressed as he could not express them himself, nor find, nor even wish them better than they are."

Jeremy Taylor, speaking of his trials during a time of civil war, and of the relief derived from these writings, says: "I found so many admirable promises, so rare variety of the expressions of the mercies of God, the commemoration of so many deliverances, that I began to be so confident as to believe that there could come no affliction great enough to spend so great a stock of comfort as was laid up in this treasury."

So Dr. Richard Hooker asks: "What is there necessary for man to know which the Psalms are not able to teach? Heroic magnanimity, exact wisdom, repentance unfeigned, unwearied patience, the mysteries of God, the comforts of grace, the works of Providence over this world, and the promised joys of the world to come, this one celestial fountain yieldeth. The choice and flower of all things profitable in other books, the Psalms do both more briefly contain and more movingly express."

These are voices of the past; and the present repeats them. Never were these inspired lyrics more dear to the children of God than they are to-day. They enter into the willing ears of childhood; they give tone and fervor to domestic and social worship; they soften the heart to penitence; they enlarge our minds with sublimer conceptions of God; they bear up the depressed spirit to a region of light and hope; all over the world congregations of worshippers repeat them, and they fall like accents of home on the stranger in a foreign land; and when the end of life draws near, read in the palace and the cottage, they give the same blessed peace. The dying statesman and the dying pauper repeat, "Though I walk through the valley of the shadow of death, I will fear no evil."

They were first heard in the caves of Engedi and on the hill-sides of Judea; the courts of the temple, crowded with worshippers, next echoed their jubilant strain; then they sounded westward, and, as the nations received the truth, they learned these songs. They came over to these shores in the Mayflower, and to-day the Pacific coast is ringing with their melody. We have sent them to Asia, to Africa, to the islands of the sea, and "they are yet to awaken the dumb millions of China and Japan." "The sweet singer of Israel has penetrated further than Alexander," and gained victories more lasting.

Besides, there are private associations connected with these Psalms which you can each recall. In your old family Bibles, many of which are legacies from the sainted dead, what pages are more thumbed and worn than those of this book? How affecting the story those pages could tell. One psalm was read in a season of grief, or of conflict, or of despondency — mayhap, upon the bended knee; another, by the sick-bed; another, at a funeral. There are the traces of tears upon another, which the bereaved shed when he was looking for consolation — nor looking in vain. Myriads, innumerable as the redeemed, have thus been quickened and comforted; and God's smile has rested on them as their affections have been brought into unison with the deep, devotional fervor of these holy songs.

If you will permit me to refer to my own experience, there is one Psalm, the sixty-third, thus made peculiarly dear. My beloved father, in the last interview I had with him, told me that when, a half century before, this Psalm was read by his father at family prayers, his own heart responded, and he felt the first conscious emotions of love to God. Then with a voice faltering through weakness, he repeated, "O God, Thou art my God; early will I seek thee. My soul thirsteth for Thee, my flesh longeth for Thee in a dry and thirsty land where no water is. Because Thy loving kindness is better than life, my lips shall praise Thee. Because Thou hast been my help, therefore in the shadow of Thy wings will I rejoice." "These words," he added, "have been very precious to me. Through them I have so often had sweet communion with God, that I feel I can trust Him now." It was his dying testimony, and you will not wonder that I often read with a throbbing heart this, which I venture to think of as "my father's Psalm."

Suffer me, then, earnestly to commend to your more constant reading and more diligent study, this portion of the inspired Word. A few verses may be obscure without explanation; but by far the greater portion needs only the commentary of a pious heart, and a mind enlightened by the Spirit. Read, to admire, if you will, the beauty of expression, the affluence of imagery, the vivacity of style; but read, more carefully to learn of the glory of God, and of His constant providence; of the universal kingdom of the Messiah, and of the wide contrast between the character and the destiny of the righteous and the wicked.

Above all, read to imbue your soul in the spirit of the holy writers. God helping you, make their words your own. Let their emotions be kindled in your breast. On the wings of their faith, with the fervor of their desire, with the animation of their gratitude, with the clearness of their vision, mount up to heaven. The effort will afford a trial of your spiritual state. "How do you like the one hundred and nineteenth Psalm?" was the test-question which a devout Christian used to put to those seeking admission to the Church. All is not right within, if there is no response felt to the tones of this sacred minstrelsy. The heart unmoved by it, would be cold and silent amid the songs of heaven.

It was a custom, we are told, of the early Christians, to learn this book by heart, that psalmody might soften the fatigues and soothe the sorrows of life. Nor is it adapted only for our hours of reflection and grief. St. James gives good advice when he says, "Is any merry? Let him sing psalms." They may sober, but will not sadden us; they can exhilerate with a higher delight than was ever felt when the brilliant drawing-room has echoed to the trills of an Italian song.

And he who truly loves these Psalms shall draw near to his end as the book itself closes, with glad rejoicings. The last five, it has been noticed, are "like the land Beulah," where the sun shineth night and day. The Psalmists, having left all their conflicts and troubles behind, seem to stand on a clear eminence, breaking forth into peans of uninterrupted joy, and calling on all above, below, around, to join in their songs. Thus do they typify the destiny of those who have followed them with devout sympathy, and who shall themselves stand forth at last, the hymns of sadness and penitence to be repeated no more, shouting the notes of everlasting praise.

Religion and Our Secular Duties.

AND THE LORD SPAKE UNTO MOSES, SAYING, SEE, I HAVE CALLED BY NAME BEZALEEL, THE SON OF URI, THE SON OF HUR, OF THE TRIBE OF JUDAH; AND I HAVE FILLED HIM WITH THE SPIRIT OF GOD, IN WISDOM, AND IN UNDERSTANDING, AND IN KNOWLEDGE, AND IN ALL MANNER OF WORKMANSHIP, TO DEVISE CUNNING WORKS, TO WORK IN GOLD, AND IN SILVER, AND IN BRASS. *Exodus*, xxxi.: 1—4.

THE peculiarity of this passage and the point where we are to find lessons of instruction is the fact the Spirit of God is recognized as preparing Bezaleel to be a skilful worker in gold, silver and brass.

This phrase, "Spirit of God," is indeed used with wider latitude in the Old Testament than in the New; still it always implies a direct Divine influence — that God fills the man with His own energy and life; that He comes down, as it were, from the height of His glory, breathes upon His creature, prepares him for a work beyond his unaided wisdom and strength.

We are fond of making a division of our actions into two classes, calling the one religious, the other secular. To the first belong, for example, prayer, worship, beneficence, words of Christian exhortation, and the various duties of the Sabbath; to the other, our labors on other days, our words in social intercourse, and our recreations. Now I do not affirm that there is no ground for this distinction, and that it never ought to be made; but I say it is made too broadly and too often, and that the great truth is kept far too much out of sight, that a cold heart may make these so-called religious acts worse than secular, while a sanctified spirit may render our most common labors religious.

The evil of insisting too rigidly on this distinction, is that it favors the idea that piety is to concern itself with and be manifested in a certain class of duties, instead of shedding its savor over the whole life. What we want is a full-orbed, symmetrical development; and any idea which limits our holy endeavors, or makes us unmindful of God in any act, is defective and injurious.

Will you, then, consider *the connection of what are called our secular acts with piety*, or, if I may so express it, the *religiousness* of these acts?

First, *these actions are all performed under the eye of God.* "Thou God seest me." "Whither shall I go from thy Spirit, or whither shall I flee from thy presence? Thou compassest my path and my lying down, and art acquainted with all my ways." God is thus omnipresent, not as an unconcerned spectator; He cares for, He weighs every act of each one of His creatures. We speak of Him as dwelling in Zion, as listening to the praises of His saints, as drawing near to us on these Sabbath days; but there is no morning when He does not come to us with the reviving dawn, no word of any wicked man which He does not hear, and no house, be it sanctuary or hovel, which He does not fill.

Yet is He not peculiarly present in a place, and at an hour, like this? He is in a special manner and for special purposes, just as we are present for special services; but God is no more fully here, than in any other spot on this wide world.

This is not a truth to be demonstrated, so much as felt. It needs no demonstration to him who admits the infinitude of God. We need only to make it a reality, that He beholds us day by day, hour by hour.

Some of you have stood on the high mountain-top at the early dawn. When the first rays struck into the window of the cottager, far down in the valley, rousing him from his slumbers, your eye followed them. You noticed the first curl of the smoke from the chimney. When he went forth to the barn you watched him; heard the distant lowing of the cattle, and the bark of the house-dogs as they welcomed their master. With friendly interest you saw him commence his labor in the field. He did not notice you; he did not think of looking up at the beetling crags high above his head; yet there were many there, intent on all his movements.

So, from a far higher elevation, commanding a far wider prospect, with an eye which searcheth all things, not in the faint haze of the morning, but as in noon-day brightness, doth God look down on all His creatures and note all their actions. They may not think of Him, but He seeth them, alike in the gray dawn and shining midday, and resplendent evening and black midnight; when they go out, when they come in; in all their studies, their labors, their bargains, their sorrows, and their joys; when a new life begins, when weary age lays down its burden, when manly strength summons itself for any struggle. Aye, O man, whoever thou art, the All-seeing Eye is upon thee always; God "understandeth thy thought afar off."

In this respect there is no distinction between different classes of our actions, or our words, or our thoughts; all alike are the objects of Divine regard.

Again: *our secular acts, like those which we call religious, are performed by the help of God.* "Without Me, ye can do nothing." "In Him we live, and move, and have our being." These assertions of Scripture know no exceptions. You can no more lift your hand without God, and put forth your strength in your daily efforts to earn your bread, than without His aid you can lift your heart to Him acceptably in prayer. The influence is not of the same kind in both cases; but in both is it equally Divine, and to be recognized as from God. Here the text comes in with the assertion, that it was through the "Spirit of God" that Bezaleel became skilful to work in gold, silver, and brass.

Is not this often forgotten? Are there not many, even of those who call themselves Christians, who do not pray with any fervency—who would feel under constraint in praying, that God would be with them in the place of labor or traffic, to put vigor in their right arms, or give them clearness of financial discernment? It seems to them as if in such matters they must depend on their own strength and their own acuteness, such as they may have; and are not to look for any increase in these respects directly from God.

But is this to "acknowledge God in all our ways, that He may direct our paths"? These powers, which we call our own; this foresight and shrewdness, and every other similar endowment, are they not from Him, as well as the loving, believing heart? If He created these powers, will He not reinforce them? Why not, then, ask Him to do so, when we are using them innocently? We may not pray for cunning to overreach another, but may we not for due sagacity? And if Christian men honored God more by thus seeking His help while they put forth their own best efforts, would they not obtain more help, and be kept from many a disaster which now comes upon them?

It is a homely but true proverb, "Prayer and provender hinder no man's journey." We may extend it: prayer hinders no work of man, but helps forward all. It is not certain that the man who prays most over his daily business will grow rich the fastest; for it may be for his real good that he should not. Yet he will be more likely to succeed; he will, in any event, conduct his affairs on right principles, and will grow in grace amid all their turmoil; and there will be constant peace and gladness in his heart, such as no increase of riches could give.

We may not, then, shut God out from any sphere of human activity. To limit His agency; to say of one class of duties, these are religious, we may seek God's aid in them, and pray over them; and then to say of another class, or even to think it, those are secular, in them we must depend upon ourselves alone, — is atheistic, dishonorable to God, enfeebling and disastrous to man.

Further: *for all our secular actions we are accountable to God, and our characters are tested in them.* Stated as an abstract truth, few will deny this; but, practically, it is kept out of sight. How many have a conscience of times and places: at certain seasons and particular localities, very careful; at others, very easy and free. They remind you of a Sabbath on the continent of Europe, occupied with apparently devout Church-going in the morning, and most undevout merrymaking in the afternoon. Now, life should be uniform in its spirit, and conscience control every act.

When judging of the character, it is true we generally appeal to such exercises as repentance, and faith, and prayer; to the feelings cherished in view of sin, of God, of the Bible, of the Cross of Christ. And we do so, because in these the state of the heart is most plainly manifested; these are exercises and emotions wherein the Christian differs most widely from the unbeliever. But if we could read the most secret workings of the mind by a glance, as God does; if we could decide accurately on the precise motive and spirit by which every action is prompted, then could we say, on viewing merely the conduct of any one at his daily tasks, or hearing his ordinary conversation, what manner of man he is.

Let the Bible instruct us on this point. It not only rebukes men for those vices which are the "works of the flesh," but, pointing to the scenes of every-day life, declares, "The plowing of the wicked is sin"; and in a great number of cases aims its denunciations at offences connected with ordinary and secular transactions. "The hire of your laborers, who have reaped down your fields, which is of you kept back by fraud, crieth; and the cries of them which have reaped have entered into the ears of the Lord of Sabaoth." "Shall I count them pure with the wicked balances, and with the bag of deceitful weights?" "Woe unto you, Scribes and Pharisees, hypocrites, for ye devour widows' houses, and for a pretence make long prayers." There, emphatically, is the judgment on those divorcing religion from common life. Their scrupulousness in acts of religious service could not avail. It was worse than useless to attempt thus to disguise their guilt. God, who cannot be mocked,— He, whose eye had followed them away from the temple, would drag to light all the transactions of those unconsecrated hours when they thought so little of Him, and these would prove their ruin.

So in that last judgment, when all these special verdicts shall be reaffirmed, and the whole life pass in review, not alone the hours passed in the sanctuary, not merely the reception given to direct warnings, shall be brought to light, but "every secret thing," "all the deeds done in the body," and men shall give account "for every idle word." How plain that the scrutiny is to be thorough, universal, unlimited by the distinctions we foolishly set up; that as no act or thought can be hidden from the knowledge of God, so none will be excepted from the inspection and awards of that solemn day.

Once more: *our secular actions are all to be performed in the remembrance of, and to the glory of God.* This is a consideration which points us down beneath the surface of things, and indicates what is to be the spirit of our lives, always of far greater consequence than their form.

To some the idea of doing all things thus, may need explanation. They see how a man can pray, or worship in the house of God, or bestow his goods on the perishing, for God's glory, but not how he can labor or amuse himself to the same end.

Precisely how, then, is a day-laborer, whose work is digging a ditch, to honor and serve God in that? He will go forth to his task acquiescing in it as God's appointment. It is not a very pleasant work; he may feel that he is capable of something higher; but if Providence has shut him up to it, he will accept the allotment cheerfully. He will not be ashamed of his position, because God has placed him in it, and, as he knows, will smile on and reward his fidelity there.

Again, he will be faithful and diligent, that he may please God. His piety will lead him to do his best. He may be laboring with no overseer, and might easily loiter and lengthen out his job, but the thought of Him who watches all our toil, will keep him from yielding to the temptation. Do you not see how that man, though his clothes may be as coarse and soiled as those of any of his companions, differs from them, and how his work is rising in dignity to a holy service?

Read his thoughts further, and see how gratitude to his Creator for the strength given, and a peaceful sense of the Divine presence fill his breast; and when he rests from his labor and receives his wages, they are devoted to such purposes as God will approve. A dependent family may claim the largest share, and the Divine blessing humbly sought will descend upon the household as they eat the daily bread, earned by that honest toil.

Has not that man been living religiously that day, even if we leave out of view all outward acts of devotion? Has he not been doing the will of God, in the very use of the implements of labor, as truly as he who may the same day have been preaching Christ, or, after the example of his Master, pouring balm into the wounds of suffering humanity?

As in toil, so in recreation, which seems at first to present a more difficult case. We settle it, in the outset, that we need to unbend and amuse ourselves, in order to keep the powers given us in a healthy and vigorous state. This being so, with a clear conscience we go to the play-ground or gymnàsium, or to the scene of social festivity; out on the ocean to be rocked by its gentle undulations, or braced by its pure breezes; forth for a ramble or a ride, through the woods or up the mountain, — in all these employments believing we have God's smile, and thankfully feeling our indebtedness to Him for all our joy.

A day given up to amusement may thus be a means of grace, a step towards the Christian's highest activity and usefulness. The ultimate end sought may be far beyond a passing joy, even the glory of God.

My meaning must be plain now, in saying that all secular actions are to be thus performed. So may we honor God in everything we do. Not by a constrained service, not by tithing out to Him hours, and portions, and acts; but by such a remembrance of Him, such seeking of His help and blessing in everything, that our whole life shall be sanctified and consciously become His life in us.

What actions are there which, in this view, may not be called religious? How plain that the divorcement of religion from things secular is unwarranted and pernicious. Our whole life is to be spent as under the eye of God, as a life of constant and entire dependence, the whole tendency and aim of which is to glorify God, and for which, in all its movements and all its details, we are to give account.

I believe we suffer because such views as these are not more generally entertained. Nothing, let me say in conclusion, would more promote our growth in grace than the endeavor to carry religion more fully into our every-day lives. Do not understand me as throwing any slight on the more special and immediate acts of devotion and piety. God forbid. My desire is only to raise our other actions up nearer to their level; not to unsanctify any work of man, but to consecrate all.

Were this attained, we should not depend so much on the Sabbath alone to bring us near to

God,—one day's good influences to undo and overcome the evil which six days of a godless and worldly life have wrought—alas, how disproportionate the odds!—but every place would be to us full of God, every work bind us to Him, every path lead heavenward.

> "We need not bid, for cloistered cell,
> Our neighbors and our work farewell,
> Nor strive to wind ourselves too high
> For sinful man beneath the sky:
>
> "The trivial round, the common task,
> Would furnish all we ought to ask;
> Room to deny ourselves; a road
> To bring us daily nearer God."

Such views would also prevent us from making fidelity in worship and sacramental observances, and such specific acts of piety, an excuse for a worldly and irreligious course in our daily walk. Are there not many who keep their conscience quiet by the performance of half their duty? They would be uneasy if they omitted their morning prayer; but having paid their tithe, they can be selfish and irritable and ungenerous through the day without concern. They feel as if their Christian profession bound them to acts of devotion, to the so-called religious acts, with a weight of obligation greater than presses on them in reference to the ordinary transactions of life.

But who has given authority to make any such discrimination? It is as much a sin, according to the Scriptures, to buy and sell in forgetfulness of God, as to restrain prayer; to have no love for our brother, as to be without love to God. When this principle shapes our conduct, our halting, inconsistent lives will assume symmetry and strength.

Lastly, these truths bring the duty of living to God close home to all. How often we hear the wretched excuse, "no time for religion." The neglecter of duty and the backsliding Christian urge that they are oppressed by cares, and seem to think the plea sufficient. It supposes that religious duties are wholly separate from secular, and so must have a season divided off from the hours engrossed by necessary labors. But all time, we now see, is for religion. It takes no more time to lift the arm laboring in the fear of God, than to do the same in the service of Satan; and the first movement of a new and consecrated life may be the most common action of toil performed in a new spirit. Now is always the accepted time; the place where we are, God's presence-chamber for us.

How far are the best Christians from living up to the true ideal of piety. They are chosen to be partakers of the life of God, to have His Spirit breathing upon them continually, to live in fellowship with Him. Yet, see them bearing their cares and sorrows alone; distressed because of sins, which He has already forgiven; looking for visits from God, when He offers to abide with them always. We are all half-infidels before the amazing fulness of the promises, and our souls but half-sanctified, because we dare not seek constant union with God. We are troubled and anxious about the form of our lives, and the kind of labors we shall perform: when all this is of no account, compared with the spirit in which we act.

Be mindful concerning this. And as you have asked God's help on the Sabbath, so seek it through the week; regarding religion not as a preparation for death, but for life; not as a burdensome duty to be postponed as long as possible, but as the very joy and free-play of the soul — as the life of life.

The Connection between
The Present and the Future Life.

FOR THIS CORRUPTIBLE MUST PUT ON INCORRUPTION, AND THIS MORTAL MUST PUT ON IMMORTALITY. I. *Corinthians*, XV.: 53.

ONE great benefit of our Saviour's advent is declared to be, that He has "brought life and immortality to light." Men had before believed in an existence beyond the grave, but their ideas had been vague and unsatisfying. Not to mention now the self-contradicting conjectures of the heathen sages, who hoped rather than believed, the views we find expressed in the Old Testament Scriptures are, for the most part, far from being either clear or animating. The future world is a place of shades, of darkness, of inactivity. "There is no wisdom, nor device, nor knowledge in the grave whither thou goest." "The grave cannot praise Thee, death cannot celebrate Thee: they that go down into the pit cannot hope for Thy truth." Even David wrote, "In death there is no remembrance of Thee; in the grave who shall give Thee thanks?" Perhaps these words are not to be taken in their literal and full force; but they show how dark a shadow rested on the minds of even good men as to the future world.

There was need of a fuller revelation. The way of salvation did not more require to be illuminated, than did the gloom of man's last resting place. The claim of the Gospel is to have dispelled the darkness. Christ hath "abolished death"; through Him the grave has been despoiled of its victory. But have Christians come into the light and embraced the truth? Is not the prevailing idea, even now, that we can know but very little concerning the life beyond the grave; that it is a state of being so very different from this, that any attempt to picture its scenes will surely lead us astray? Are there not many who, on principle, forbid themselves to form any conceptions concerning it, save the general one that it will be a state of happiness and purity? Whence that happiness will spring, how their piety will employ itself, are questions they dare not ask. Perverting and curtailing a passage of Scripture, referring to provisions of mercy, beyond man's natural ken, but revealed through the Spirit, they repeat concerning heaven, as if it were a precious promise: "Eye hath not seen, nor ear heard, neither have entered the heart of man, the things which God hath prepared for them that love Him." They forget that it is added, "but God hath revealed them unto us through the Spirit."

As "all Scripture is profitable for instruction," so the neglect of any portion must be an injury; and to this general indefiniteness of view we ascribe, in part at least, the sad and strange fact that, while the doctrine of immortality is most grand and impressive, it is so inoperative. Men say that they believe that after death succeeds an infinite eternity of joy or woe; yet they live as if this world furnished the highest good, and banish the future from their thoughts. Or, if they speak of the glories of heaven, it is with a chilling apathy which belies their words.

Not so was it with those of the primitive age. Their "conversation was in heaven," from whence they looked for the Saviour, who should, "change their vile body, that it might be fashioned like unto His glorious body." They were in an attitude of eager expectation, "hasting unto the coming of the day of God." While in this tabernacle they "did groan, being burdened"; "not for that they would be unclothed, but clothed upon, that mortality might be swallowed up of life." The future was as real to them, and in many of its aspects as vividly discerned, as this present world.

If we would come back to their position, we must dismiss the idea that we can know nothing of the future except vaguely; we must not think of the soul as breaking away at death from all old habits, associations, pursuits, and modes of existence, and starting afresh upon an independent course; we must keep in mind that we retain our identity, our bodies in a changed form, our mental and moral powers, our past stores of knowledge and experience, and the characters which have been developed here. So that, to express the truth in a word, the future life is not so much a new life as a continuation of the present one: our existence being one connected whole, from the birth-hour on earth to the endless ages of futurity. Death is the extinction of the life of the mortal body, but not even an interruption of the life of the soul.

We do not mean, of course, that the future state is not in some respects different from this. We believe it a far more exalted and enlarged state of being; yet the differences are not so great as to destroy the undivided unity of our lives. The traveller may sail across an unknown sea and enter a land where the forms of nature and habits of men may be very strange; he may learn a language he never spoke before; he may change his dress, and adopt new modes of living; a torrid climate may bronze his complexion and crisp his hair; his whole appearance may be altered; yet he will be the same, linked by memory and consciousness to his past life; and no outward changes, however great, however prolonged, can sever his life in twain. So in entering the world of spirits, we cross a trackless sea, we change our dress, — for the body is the covering of the soul, — our mode of life is novel; but why suppose that in all this we lose our identity, or are any more severed from our former selves than is the traveller in Asiatic or African wilds?

> "The child 's included in the man,
> And part of him forever;
> The Past still in the Future lives,
> And basis to its being gives:
> Not it, but *of* it ever."

But let us look more closely at some of the points of contact between this and the future life.

First, *there is an intimate relation between these natural bodies which now clothe us and the spiritual bodies we shall have at the resurrection.* It is not necessary to enter on the mysteries of this subject, nor to attempt an answer to the inquiries which curiosity may suggest. We are not endeavoring to draw any "physical theory of another life," but to present the facts which the Scriptures make known.

We stand, therefore, on the simple, explicit declaration of Paul: "There is a natural body, and there is a spiritual body." What that spiritual body is, what its form, what its functions, what its glory, we need not say: but it is something. Even if we cannot describe it, we may not think it indescribable — still less, regard it as a nonentity.

"There is a spiritual body," and it has a close connection with this body of flesh. Here, again, we have direct testimony. The whole course of thought in the fifteenth chapter of the first epistle to the Corinthians, implies the reviving of that which had died. "This corruptible must put on incorruption, and this mortal must put on immortality." "It is sown in dishonor, it is raised in glory; it is sown in weakness, it is raised in power; it is sown a natural body, it is raised a spiritual body." Again, the same writer speaks of the "changing" of "these vile bodies," and the making them "like unto Christ's glorious body." Notice, their changing, not their destruction, and the formation of a body entirely new.

Other Scriptures declare that "all that are in the graves shall hear His voice, and shall come forth," and that "the sea" is to give up "the dead that are in it."

Christ's resurrection is also represented as the type and pledge of ours. He is the "first fruits." "He which raised up the Lord Jesus, shall raise up us also by Jesus." He came from the sepulchre with the same body which was crucified; upon it was visible still the print of the nails and the spear; and that same body He bore upward with Him when He ascended, — changed, probably, as when, on the mount of transfiguration, "His face did shine as the sun."

So shall these bodies of ours be transfigured. We shall not, in the future, be unclothed spirits, as, perhaps, the angels are; we shall have coverings, not gross, not fleshly, but spiritual, like a raiment of light. It is natural to believe that they will be under the more perfect control of the soul, capable of quicker motion, of a more interior and complete discernment, of unwearied endurance: in a word, they shall be the fitting vehicle and instrument of the expanding spirit.

The thought is animating. I am travelling to eternity, not with my soul merely, but this flesh shall be changed to an immortal substance. Though this be a tenement of crumbling clay, the germ of that which shall forever abide is hidden somewhere here. Members that have fulfilled their office may perish; but a body springing from this, and clothing the soul, is according to the eternal law of my being.

Secondly, *there is reason to believe that our mental actions in the future state will be similar to what they are here.*

There may be some acts — those, for example, connected with sensation — which must cease, or be greatly modified; but, in general, the common movements of the mind may go on. God delights to carry one plan of action through all ages and all worlds; and it is most like Him to perpetuate the original laws of mental action, while the mind itself endures.

Besides, there is no evidence that death has any direct power over the mind. Sometimes, indeed, the faculties seem benumbed at its approach; but at other times, and I think more frequently, the soul works clearly, powerfully to the very end, maintaining a full self-possession even after the body is, in fact, partially dead. Or when the clouds have gathered thickly, they suddenly part for a moment; the eye of the dying, which we thought was closed forever, brightens to life again, and one last emphatic word shows us that behind the clouds is the undimmed radiance of a deathless spirit.*

Now we say, not only that death does not impair the integrity of the soul but that it lives on with the same faculties as before, working in the same way, though, doubtless, with far augmented celerity and power.

Take as an illustration of this, the faculty of memory. It is common to us all, one of the most peculiar and important of our powers, having relations to our whole mind and life. It begins its operations in our earliest days, and to the close of our earthly course it is constantly collecting and storing away innumerable facts and truths. Sometimes its treasures are hidden for years, are apparently lost and then suddenly brought to light,

* A striking confirmation of this is afforded in the recently published narrative of the last hours of Dr. Hubbard Winslow. To a friend near his bedside, he said: "I stand on the verge of two worlds, with a clear consciousness of both. The separation between the two seems like an undefinable and almost undiscernible line. I am not certain that I shall be conscious when I have passed it." Again: "Do not give me anything to produce stupor, I want my mind clear. I want to be conscious when death comes." At sunrise the next morning, the morning of the day on which he died, he said, "Wheel me to the window, that I may see this glorious sight once more. I want to take the memory of these mountains into eternity with me." It is added by the one who reports this, "He seemed, in fact, to live equally in both worlds at the same time."

and so it holds them with firm tenacity to the very end of life.

Now we go farther: memory carries all its accumulations to the future world. There is no evidence, even presumptive, to the contrary; there is evidence, in what is revealed, that it will be so. Recall what is said concerning the judgment. What are those "secret things" that shall be "brought to light," but the remembered scenes and transactions of earth? How shall the award be approved by the conscience of each, save as the actions of the past come back in all their original distinctness? "Son, remember," were the words addressed to the condemned rich man in the narrative of Christ; and so from the memory will be drawn the material for future joy or woe. With power of recollection augmented, there will be arrayed before us all the scenes, the deeds, the emotions, the thoughts, of our whole lifetime. Every day, every hour, will reappear. As now we walk among the images of the past, so shall it be forever: memory will people the place of our eternal sojourn with the forms we have grown familiar with below.

We cannot refer to other faculties in detail; nor is it necessary. As the bones of the skeleton constitute a system, so that the anatomist having one can infer and construct the whole; so is there such a relation among all the powers of the mind — such symmetry of combination, that when one is found to survive unchanged, unimpaired, we are warranted in inferring that the rest are still joined with it.

It is only needful to say in a word, therefore, that all the scriptural representations of the future state exhibit the operation of other powers and emotions like those experienced here. The affections survive, and provision is made for the gratification of our social desires; they who come from the east and the west "sit down with Abraham, and Isaac and Jacob, in the kingdom of heaven;" those whom the earnest apostle has led to Christ are his "crown of rejoicing" as they meet in heaven, and the Redeemer is still the common object of love and praise. So are we pointed on to that world where the angels "desire to look into" the mysteries of redemption for the gratification of that thirst for knowledge which finds only a partial satisfaction here; "now we see through a glass darkly, but then face to face; now I know in part, but then shall I know even as also I am known." Gratitude, reverence, devotion, submission speak out in the chorus of the skies in earthly style, only with a deeper emphasis. While much is hidden, enough is revealed to make us feel that we shall be at home amid the society and employments of heaven; that our future life, though higher, intenser, will be a life marked by movements similar in kind to those familiar to us here. We shall be human still; humanity will be exalted, quickened, but not destroyed; as there is no transmigration so there will be no transfusion of souls; we shall not be mixed with beings of another race, but shall be immortal as men.

Thirdly, *the Scriptures teach that the character we form here, will remain our character forever.*

This world is constantly presented as a place of probation and of preparation for that which is to come. After death is the judgment, when men shall "give account of all the deeds done in the body" and shall receive accordingly. We are taught that there will be two classes in the future as in the present world, the friends and the enemies of God; and the conduct here will determine to which class each shall belong, and with which each shall have his eternal abode. "He that is unjust, let him be unjust still; he that is righteous, let him be righteous still."

There may be a perfecting of the work of sanctification begun before; but there is not a single promise of regeneration beyond the grave. As if all depended on our present action, men are called to choose life to-day, and warned against postponement; they are told of those who slumbered at the bridegroom's calling, and afterwards found the door shut, and cried in vain for its re-opening. The whole stress of the Gospel is to lead men to "work while the day lasts, because the night cometh, wherein no man can work."

The character, then, which we form on earth, under the varied discipline of life and the gracious influences which surround us, which we yield to, or resist; this character, as to its essential features and governing motive, we carry with us into the future world. If we would enter heaven, we must here, by the grace of God, become "meet for the inheritance of the saints in light," by extirpating all base and selfish passions and by cultivating those emotions of purity and love, those aspirations after holiness which ennoble the blessed. We must understand also, that if here we give way to malignant desires unchecked, then in the future, they will continue to burn and rage, and so make our perdition sure.

The law of the future assignment is the law of congeniality. Each goes "to his own place." Like draws to like. We need suppose no arbitrary and forced sundering of one from another: let each fall by a moral gravitation to those of congenial temper, and they who love God will be ranged with Him; they who have never submitted will be found with him who led the first rebellion.

Then restraints will be removed. From the good, those impediments will be taken by which their course was hindered, so that they seemed faithless to Him whom they truly and supremely loved; from the evil, those checks by which their passions were kept down, and wickedness avoided, into which, left to themselves, they would have plunged. The character of each will sweep on to its appropriate development in an entire and holy consecration, or in an audacious and unqualified defiance.

Thus, as was said at the commencement, is the whole theory of another life wrapped up in this one idea: *the future, — a continuation of the present.* Death changes the place, in some respects, the mode of existence, but not its nature. We shall be the same, conscious of our personal identity; bodies will still clothe and serve our spirits; our minds will be active, our affections glowing, our consciences watchful, our wills free, as here; the scenes of the past will abide with us, the character formed here be fixed and unchanging forever. Our life, divided by no chasm, renovated by no re-creation, will flow on as the stream from the fountain, broken by a sudden, precipitous fall; but flowing on, the same stream, its waters clear or perturbed beyond the fall according as they were clear or turbid before.

In closing, we would indicate some of the advantages resulting from this view of the truth.

One is, *that it makes the future state of the blessed seem more real and more attractive.* It is not necessary to repeat how far we have fallen away from the ardor of desire, and eager anticipation of heaven, cherished in the primitive age of Christianity. Dr. Chalmers too truly describes the common imagination of Paradise, as that of a "region where the inmates float in ether, or are mysteriously suspended upon nothing; where all the warm and sensible accompaniments, which give such an expression of strength and life and coloring to our present habitation, are attenuated into a sort of spiritual element, that is meagre and imperceptible, and utterly uninviting; where nothing is left, but unearthly scenes that have no power of allurement, and certain unearthly ecstasies, with which it is impossible to sympathize."

Does not the Bible teach us more than this? Did not the apostles, and may not we, behold scenes of glory which have some definiteness and reality? We sing of a "happy land, far, far away"; but, if the view we have been taking is correct, heaven begins below, and celestial joy, in its essential elements, is experienced here. The sense of forgiven sin, of a conscience pacified, of a will subdued; the glimpse of the face of a reconciled Father; the confidence which anchors the spirit when the billows roll; the rapturous gush of thankfulness and love; the bliss of serving; the delight of seeing the growing honors of our King; the hope which springs exulting at the glorious prospect; the "peace which passeth understanding," that descends like a benediction from God: are not these emotions heavenly? Must they not continue to bless the soul, and constitute the riches of the heritage of the saints? We know the song which the redeemed sing above: do we not rehearse it in our feebler way on earth? When, with swelling heart and streaming eyes, we praise Him who died for us, are not our rejoicing and thanksgiving foretastes of that which is to come? And, as here we thus anticipate heaven, shall we not there look back on these glad hours as having been the dawning of that immortal day?

Away, then, with that timidity, so fearful of going beyond what is revealed that it loses the comfort and strength God has provided. Let the infidel speak of death as "a leap in the dark," but let the Christian, feeling that the grave has lost its victory, depart with the cheerfulness with which he would cross the ocean, knowing that friends were waiting on the farther shore; greater wonders than he had ever seen were there to be disclosed; his powers find higher employment, and the longing of his life-time be at last fulfilled. Nay, death is not a distant voyage; it is stepping across a rill. In one moment its work is done; and it is conceivable that one should commence a song of praise on earth and finish that same strain in the immediate presence of God.

Another use of this view of truth is, *to show the reasonableness of the doctrine of future retribution.* As the bliss of heaven begins on earth, so have transgressors also a foretaste of at least some of the elements of the misery of hell. When we would know what is their doom, we need not with busy fancy conjure up imagined sufferings, unlike all known below; but may think of the shame of detected sin, of the raging of unsatisfied desire, of the upbraidings of an awakened conscience, of the remorse which pursues the guilty, making the day oppressive, and the night hideous; of that agonizing, crushing sense, which some have felt, of abandonment by God, when there seemed none to hear and pity, and none to save; and by such dreadful experiences, which not all the wealth or glory of the world could render tolerable, we may know what is the portion of those, to whom the Judge will say, "Depart." Depart with all the burden of unforgiven sin; with all the memories of the past to haunt you; with conscience active, and no flattering voice to deny its accusations. Depart, from the presence of all the good, from My smile and favor, to dwell with those who are filled with hatred and unrighteousness, in "the outer darkness."

There is nothing strange, nothing unnatural, in such inflictions; such are the normal consequences of sin, to be expected, unless our nature, or our characters are changed. God does thus visit men, to show them of what suffering they are capable; to warn them that perdition is near, that they carry its germs in their own bosoms. The burden of proof is on those who deny retribution. They are to show some express declaration that the laws of our being have been reversed; and that despite all experience here, one can sin and still dwell in peace.

Finally, *this view invests all the actions and labors of this life with peculiar interest and dignity.* It is not within our option whether or not we will prepare for the life to come: by the fixed laws of our being, we must do so. We are to meet every act of ours at the judgment: we shall retain in our sensitive minds even the impression of every thought. They who have sowed sparingly will reap sparingly; while —

> "The more our spirits are enlarged on earth,
> The deeper draughts shall they receive of heaven."

No labor is lost; no step of real advancement is in vain. There will be a personal individuality in the future, as now. When one has enriched his soul with generous sympathies, and feels an absorbing interest in the progress of truth and the triumph of right, he will be thus prepared to rejoice more than others at the unfolding of the vast plans of God. He whose heart has expanded on earth with the warmest love for Christ will gaze with the liveliest rapture at His unveiled glory. May not even one of sanctified and developed intellect start on his future career with an advantage gained from his attainments below? Every mental, every moral power given, we are to use in God's service: while these powers endure, He will find them employment; and we may be sure, from the analogy of His usual method, that no true development of them will be thrown away.

How strong a motive to fidelity in the use of every power, every opportunity. Let not a day be unimproved. By an inevitable law we are constantly shaping our future; every hour are storing up material for unending joy or woe. That unseen world is not distant, it touches this. Why let our vision be bounded by the narrow horizon of earth? In the twinkling of an eye, at the lifting of a vail, the stupendous scenes of eternity may appear; and we, with mental and moral powers and characters as now, remembering the past, unchanged as to our essential being, shall stand before God.

Go with a Pastor's blessing,
  Tell of Redeeming love,
Speak to each weary pilgrim
  Of rest and joy above.
Declare the Spirit's mission,
  The burdened heart to cheer;
A heavenly peace He bringeth,
  Relief from every fear.

Bid every fainting Christian
  A sweet assurance seek;
Our Lord is all compassion,
  He loves to aid the weak.
With holy zeal untiring,
  Bid every child of God
Press onward in the pathway
  His earnest Master trod.

O'er each day's life may Jesus
  His hallowed influence shed;
With reverent, trustful spirit
  The sacred Word be read;
Then sinless souls rejoicing,
  Before the throne shall stand,
All care, all grief forgotten,
  Safe in the better land.

C. A. M.

www.ingramcontent.com/pod-product-compliance
Lightning Source LLC
LaVergne TN
LVHW021422110826
845150LV00007B/2040
* 9 7 8 1 4 2 5 5 0 8 9 5 1 *